Socrates' Muse:
Reflections on Effective
Case Discussion Leadership

Robert F. Bruner
Darden Graduate School of Business and
The Batten Institute
University of Virginia

McGraw-Hill
Irwin

Boston   Burr Ridge, IL   Dubuque, IA   Madison, WI   New York   San Francisco   St. Louis
Bangkok   Bogotá   Caracas   Kuala Lumpur   Lisbon   London   Madrid   Mexico City
Milan   Montreal   New Delhi   Santiago   Seoul   Singapore   Sydney   Taipei   Toronto

McGraw-Hill Higher Education

*A Division of The **McGraw·Hill** Companies*

SOCRATES' MUSE: REFLECTIONS ON EFFECTIVE CASE DISCUSSION LEADERSHIP
Robert F. Bruner

Published by McGraw-Hill/Irwin, an imprint of the McGraw-Hill Companies, Inc., 1221 Avenue of the Americas, New York, NY 10020.

2 3 4 5 6 7 8 9 0 HAM/HAM 0 9 8 7 6 5 4 3 2

ISBN 0-07-248566-3

www.mhhe.com

In Dedication
To the memory of

C. Roland Christensen

He was Robert Walmsley University Professor, Harvard University where he led faculty seminars on teaching at the Business School from 1970 to 1993 and taught business policy from 1947. Teachers should remember him for his visionary leadership that helped to elevate faculty discourse about classroom teaching at Harvard, and particularly about the discussion method of teaching. He and his team became an example for other universities and an inspiration for individual instructors around the world. He often said that teaching was like sending a letter with an imperfect address: you never knew where and when the message would be delivered. I believe his message will continue to be delivered widely for some time to come.

It was my privilege to study with him and to serve briefly as his research assistant. Under his guidance, I wrote my first case study, "Real Paper Inc. (A)." I found him to be patient, kindly, and highly professional—all motivated by a strong vision. His supervisory method was a blend of questioning and editorial commentary salted with anecdotes, poetry, and personal advice. He was a major positive influence on my decision to become an academician. I offer this book to his memory in gratitude.

-- RFB

Foreword

Louis B. Barnes
John D. Black Professor Emeritus
Professor of Organizational Behavior Emeritus
Harvard Business School

Good books with a *student-learning* perspective are rare. More often, academic writers display their knowledge and research (journal) concerns along with their discipline orientations, rather than addressing student-learning issues.

But this is one of those rare books, intended for teachers who really *care* about student learning. Building initially upon his own MBA student experiences and upon later work as a case writer for our mutual mentor, Professor C. Roland Christensen at Harvard, Bob Bruner went on to mine even deeper teaching-and-learning veins as a distinguished professor at the University of Virginia's Darden Graduate School of Business.

More importantly, this book demonstrates Bruner's concern for students, and their active learning processes. He approaches classroom leadership using case studies as the primary vehicle for interactive student-centered dialogues. His approach to teaching begins with five initial core-value concepts, and any teacher would do well to use them as bases for the implicit learning contracts that get established in every classroom. Those initial value concepts for teachers are:

- Ask often, tell seldom.
- Begin one's teaching and course design from *the perspective of the student.*
- Exercise students' judgment, because it builds wisdom.
- Research builds renewal.
- The task of the teacher is to help the student "make meaning."

For many university professors, these values are, if not counter-intuitive, at least contrary to the conventional wisdoms of instructor control and solid lecture presentations. Bruner begins with a very different assumption; that real learning begins only when a concerned, inquiring teacher helps to unleash *active* student minds and ideas in a learning process that comes out of good classroom dialogue. Those classroom questions and dialogues become the keys to active learning, as the facilitating instructor; 1) asks more questions and gives fewer answers, 2) builds a course that begins with student a perspective, 3) draws out student judgments (not just 'answers") as a way toward developing individual wisdom, 4) Uses research as a way to build renewal as well as knowledge, and 5) works to help students "make" their own meaning out of discussion experiences. Such a facilitating instructor has begun to understand Bruner's notion of Socrates' Muse – and to its role in effective case discussion leadership.

But, as the author declares, this is more than a book on pedagogical values. It is a "how-to" book for teachers who want to use its core values as springboards to practice everything from coping with silent students to turning "mindless" students into "mindful" learners. Its chapters address topics ranging from humor in the classroom to coping with silent students to helping a class discussion "catch fire."

It is clear that Bruner enjoys working with the ideas he presents in the book. I suspect that the reader will enjoy them even more.

Louis B. Barnes
May 2002
Boston, Massachusetts

About the Author

Robert F. Bruner is Distinguished Professor of Business Administration and Executive Director of the Batten Institute at the Darden Graduate School of Business Administration, University of Virginia, where he has served on the faculty since 1982. His research in corporate finance has been published in journals such as *Financial Management, Journal of Accounting and Economics, Journal of Applied Finance, Journal of Applied Corporate Finance, Journal of Financial Economics, Journal of Financial and Quantitative Analysis,* and *Journal of Money, Credit, and Banking.* His current research addresses issues in mergers and acquisitions, corporate finance, and valuation of assets in emerging markets. He is founding co-editor of *Emerging Markets Review.* Since 2000, he has directed the Batten Institute, which sponsors applied research and knowledge transfer programs in the areas of innovation and business change.

He teaches corporate financed in Darden's MBA program and at various other institutions. He has received numerous awards for teaching and for his teaching materials, including the highest teaching awards from the University of Virginia, and the State of Virginia. *Business Week* magazine cited him as one of the "masters of the MBA classroom." He is the author of over 400 items of teaching material, and of *Case Studies in Finance: Managing for Corporate Value Creation* (McGraw-Hill/Irwin) now in its fourth edition. He is founding co-editor of *Educator: Courses, Cases & Teaching*, an electronic journal that discusses teaching materials and techniques in the field of finance. Industrial corporations, financial institutions, and government agencies have retained him for counsel and training.

He has served the Darden School, professional groups, and community organizations in various positions of leadership. In 2002 the Financial Management Association elected him its Vice President—Education. He holds the B.A. from Yale University, and the M.B.A., and D.B.A. from Harvard University. His web site is http://faculty.darden.edu/brunerb/. He may be contacted by email at brunerr@virginia.edu.

Preface

The title of this book, *Socrates' Muse*, suggests my aims. First, the reference to Socrates highlights the book's focus: teaching by means of dialogue. He is one of the godparents of discussion-based teaching, and is interesting to teachers as an example of how to teach. This is a "how-to" book. Second, the reference to a muse, or creative alter ego, hypothesizes that the teacher might reflect on the discussion enterprise, as a basis for the teacher's own learning, and for improving the learning of one's students. Self-reflection to reason through the challenges of discussion leadership is an important attribute of the teaching professional.

The mission of this work is to help university-level instructors promote more effective professional learning by students through discussions. Consider some of the elements of this mission:

- **Explore what it means to teach by discussion leadership.** I will emphasize how effective discussion leadership entails *asking* rather than telling. To an instructor, steeped in knowledge of a field, this will seem counterintuitive. In large part, this book is oriented toward the *transformation of the instructor*.

- **Focus on higher education with a professional orientation.** While the tips here are easily extended to primary and secondary education, the book assumes a high level of student maturity, motivation, and cognitive development. The challenges of higher education warrant a focused discussion. Discussion-based training (e.g., in seminars and tutorials) permeates university life. I draw a frame of reference mainly to professional fields first because of my direct personal experience there (I teach at a graduate business school and have taught occasionally at a law school) and second because of the renewed focus on the quality of learning experience in many of those fields. I hope this book lends traction to the movement to improve professional training.

- **Consider a range of possible teaching materials, but emphasize case studies.** One can lead a discussion about virtually anything, including a textbook chapter, a website, a poem, newspaper clippings, or lab bench results. I focus somewhat on case studies because they represent professional life better than most other kinds of teaching materials. Cases convey the messiness and ambiguities of professional dilemmas, the blind alleys of analysis, and the need to extract an insight or make a decision. Teachers in fields such as law, medicine, and business use case studies as the unit of study. The insights relevant to teaching with case studies are readily applicable to other kinds of teaching materials.

- **Focus on learning, not teaching.** Teaching is but a means to an end. I believe that the point of the classroom enterprise should be deep learning, i.e., growth in knowledge and wisdom, not merely acquisition of information. To achieve this, the instructor needs a student-centered point of view: a perspective on who the learner is, and how he or she makes meaning of the subject of the course.

Origins of this book

I wrote this to serve as a source to which the discussion leader could turn for practical ideas. I believed that such a work could help colleagues in at least five ways:

- **Frame the task.** Simply knowing how to get started as a discussion leader is a major hurdle. I argue that "getting started" begins well before the first class meeting and entails careful reflection on the students' learning opportunities and challenges. Several of the chapters in this book stimulate the reflection process necessary to framing the task of discussion leadership.

- **Link the task to some deeper issues.** For every "how" there must be a "why." Readers of my case studies and the teaching-oriented journal that I co-edit send queries seeking advice on a range of teaching issues. I try to respond, but within the limits of email can offer only limited suggestions. More effective response to teaching challenges must reach deeper into why one teaches by the case method, how one organizes, how one creates a learning culture, and so on—all plainly beyond the scope of a short note but vitally important to effective discussion leadership. I sought to link techniques of discussion leadership to these deeper issues.

- **Make sense of the quest for effectiveness.** I argue that good teaching arises from more than luck or gimmicks, and that however difficult your discussion leadership experience has been, you *can* learn to teach well. I have made a number of the mistakes mentioned in this book, and profited from reflection upon them. What gave meaning to the errors and frustrations was the sense that I was engaged in a search for good teaching techniques that would ultimately promote better learning among students. Perhaps this outlook will serve you as well.

- **Capture the oral tradition.** I remember faculty lunches at the Darden School years ago, where colleagues would gather to chat about their work. Inevitably, the talk turned to teaching. As a novice instructor, I found these informal discussions to be enormously helpful. They were friendly, brief, and loaded with practical tips. In today's 24/7 economy, we have less time for this kind of exchange. I wanted to capture the intellectual capital of those conversations and perhaps rekindle a spirit of collegial dialogue about the classroom craft.

- **Extend the literature.** The discussion leader has a relatively small literature on which to draw for counsel. My intent was to complement the sound recent literature[1] on case discussion leadership and to bring into focus some practical issues.

This may seem like a mere *self-improvement* book, the kind of literature that serious scholars richly avoid. That is a misperception. Embedded here among the details about what successful discussion leaders do is a *philosophy* of discussion leadership. This book is offers an intellectual mosaic. To see it, one must study the particles, and then step back to absorb the whole. Be an empiricist. Consider this book as an exercise in inductive research devoted to forming your own philosophy about discussion leadership. Read each chapter here as a discussion at two levels: (a) the details about what to do in the classroom and (b) the larger point of view.

This book offers three short case studies to stimulate the reader's learning by the very process of student-centered discovery that I advocate. These cases give a taste of the classroom but, ultimately, one learns teaching by doing. The teacher's laboratory is the classroom, not the armchair. Most of this book is written in a directive style, rather like a collection of *technical notes*[2] that outline tools and concepts for practical use. The directive style is offered to help accelerate the instructor's transition from the armchair to the classroom, from lecture to discussion leadership, from reflection to action. The brevity of these notes follows the advice of the King of Hearts in *Alice in Wonderland*: "Start at the beginning. And when you come to the end, stop." Such has been the formula for successful teaching resources such as Rilke's *Letters to a Young Poet*, Idries Shah's *The Way of the Sufi,* or Bloom's *How to Read a Book and Why*. They show that brevity can serve the reader well.

---

[1] I recommend two contemporary books to the reader who is interested in discussion leadership. See Louis B. Barnes, C. Roland Christensen, and Abby J. Hansen, *Teaching and the Case Method*, 3rd ed., Boston: Harvard Business School Press, 1994; and C. Roland Christensen, David A. Garvin, and Ann Sweet (eds.) *Education for Judgment: The Artistry of Discussion Leadership*, Boston: Harvard Business School Press, 1991.

[2] Case studies are occasionally augmented by technical notes that present tools or concepts for possible use by the student in defining or resolving the problems in the case.

It might be objected that teaching is a *craft*, not even an art, and certainly not a science. Crafts are dominated by *tacit knowledge,* the kind developed either by personal trial-and-error, or by observing a Master and repeating the Master's actions. According to this view, one cannot become a good teacher through book learning. I believe that case teaching *is* knowable and that one can learn it and teach others how to teach better. This book can help prepare one for observation, practice, experimentation, and teaching others.

In short, I invite the reader to engage the book as a guided exploration for the reader, as an introduction (rather than conclusion), and as an exercise in the acquisition of a craft.

Sources and Acknowledgments

This volume assembles a blend of completely new work (about one-third of the book), and previous writings.[3] The earlier material is drawn from memos and technical notes for use at Darden, and from my columns in the electronic journal *Educator: Cases, Courses, & Teaching*[4], which I co-edit with Peter Tufano and Kent Womack. I have revised and expanded this earlier material to reflect numerous conversations, written exchanges, and my current thinking. All of the material reflects the criticisms of several colleagues who read one or more drafts:

- **Marva Barnett** is Professor in the College of the Arts and Sciences, and Director of the Teaching Resource Center at University of Virginia, http://trc.virginia.edu. Through word and deed, her exceptional leadership has inspired university instructors across Virginia to reflect on teaching and to improve their skills.

- **Barbara McTigue Bruner, Ph.D.,** has studied cases at Harvard, and taught by the discussion method at the University of Virginia's Darden Graduate School of Business Administration and the McIntire School of Commerce. Today she stands outside of the daily clatter of academic life, and thereby brought a valuable perspective to the reading of the manuscript. She is my fondest critic, and my wife.

---

[3] The following three chapters are published here by the kind permission of the copyright holder, the Trustees of the University of Virginia Darden School Foundation: "This Isn't Starting the Way I Wanted," UVA-G-0562 (Chapter 2); "Introduction to the Teaching Portfolio," UVA-G-0556 (incorporated into Chapter 18); and "Note to the Student: How to Study and Discuss Cases," UVA-G-0563 (the appendix to Chapter 24). Loose-leaf copies of these materials may be obtained by writing to dardencases@virginia.edu.

[4] This journal is published by Social Science Research Network, found at www.ssrn.com.

- **James G. Clawson** is a teacher of teachers, and writer on teaching by the discussion method. He is Professor of Business Administration at Darden where he leads courses in leadership, organizational behavior, and career management.

- **Jessica Chan** is Research Assistant at Darden where she has written and revised numerous case studies. As an MBA graduate of Darden, she has been a keen student of discussion leadership styles.

- **Marcia Conner** is the Executive Director for The Learnativity Alliance, a small research institute and advisory services practice. The Alliance provides a venue for members to access and share new research and best practices about adult learning, knowledge creation, talent development, and human capital management. She also serves as Editor-in-Chief of *Learning in the New Economy Magazine* and manages www.Learnativity.com.

- **Robert D. Landel** is the Henry E. McWane Professor of Business Administration. He teaches courses in operations management, innovation, manufacturing management, and systems thinking in The Darden School's MBA program. As former Associate Dean for the MBA Program, he stimulated my early writings on case teaching.

- **Douglas L. Leslie** is Charles O. Gregory Professor of Law and Thomas F. Bergin Teaching Professor of Law at the University of Virginia School of Law, and an articulate advocate of discussion-based teaching in law schools. He is engaged in creating a case discussion literature in law based on problems to be solved by students. One can see a description of Leslie's approach at www.CaseFileMethod.com.

- **Michael L. Schill** is Assistant Professor of Business Administration at Darden. I first met him as an MBA student at INSEAD. There, he developed a case study with me, and has gone on to write others. His perspective as a junior colleague has been especially helpful.

- **William W. Sihler, Jr.,** is Ronald E. Trzcinski Professor of Business Administration teaches in the Finance area at Darden. He counseled me as a mentor during my early years in the profession, and remains an outstanding guide for discussion leaders.

- **Elliott N. Weiss** is Isidore Horween Research Professor of Business Administration and Associate Dean for MBA Education. A friend and muse about discussion leadership, he is a teacher of teachers at Darden.

They have my deep thanks for their detailed and penetrating criticism. Some of their suggestions will require a subsequent edition to fulfill.

I extend sincere thanks to many people with whose counsel and encouragement this book became possible. Michele Janicek, my editor at McGraw-Hill/Irwin, was an early proponent of the project. Her sponsorship was the trigger for action. Indirectly, this book reflects wisdom of teaching exemplars from whom I have benefited over the years, including Tony Athos, Marjorie W. Bruner, C. Roland Christensen, Peter J. Gomes, John H. McArthur, David W. Mullins, Jr., and William W. Sihler, Jr. My co-editors at *Educator* lent encouragement and stimulating exchange over the years—they have included Steve Kaplan of the University of Chicago, Peter Tufano of Harvard, Kent Womack of Dartmouth, and Karen Wruck of Ohio State. Colleagues at Darden and elsewhere contributed importantly but less directly to my thinking about case discussion leadership.

Cheryl Adams, Darden	Ed Davis, Darden	Gabriel Hawawini, INSEAD
Raj Aggarwal, John Carroll	Kees Dekluyver, Claremont	Peter Hedlund, Darden
Donald Aielli, Darden	Jean Dermine, INSEAD	Rocky Higgins, Washington
Brandt Allen, Darden	Michael Dooley, UVA Law	Alec Horniman, Darden
Melissa Appleyard, Darden	Bernard Dumas, INSEAD	John Hund, Texas
Paul Asquith, MIT	Ken Eades, Darden	Lynn Isabella, Darden
By Barnes, Harvard	Mark Eaker, Darden	David Jemison, UT-Austin
Alan Beckenstein, Darden	Richard Ellsworth, Claremont	Michael Jensen, Harvard and Monitor
Gary Blemaster, Georgetown	Javier Estrada, IESE	Sreeni Kamma, Indiana
Sam Bodily, Darden	Ben Esty, Harvard	Steve Kaplan, Chicago
Karl-Adam Bonnier, Sweden	Bob Fair, Darden	Karen Marsh King, Darden
John Boquist, Indiana	Greg Fairchild, Darden	Andrew Karolyi, Ohio State
Jay Bourgeois, Darden	Paul Farris, Darden	Carl Kester, Harvard
Andrew Boynton, IMD	Pablo Fernandez, IESE	Dan Laughhunn, Duke
Duke Bristow, UCLA	Debbie Fisher, Darden	Herwig Langohr, INSEAD
Bliss Browne, Imagine Chicago	Ginny Fisher, Darden	Andrea Larson, Darden
Dick Brownlee, Darden	Stephen Foerster, IVEY	Richard Linowes, American
Kirt Butler, Michigan State	Ted Forbes, Darden	Chris Lehmbeck, Darden
Jordi Canals, IESE	Gunther Franke, Konstanz	Jeanne Liedtka, Darden
Mari Capestany, Enron	Jim Freeland, Darden	Dennis Logue, Oklahoma
Robert Carraway, Darden	Ed Freeman, Darden	Will Luckert, Darden
Don Chance, VPI&SU	Sherwood Frey, Darden	Luann Lynch, Darden
Susan Chaplinsky, Darden	Bill Fulmer, George Mason	Tom Macavoy, Darden
Ming-Jer Chen, Darden	Jim Gentry, Illinois	Wesley Marple, Northeastern
Petra Christmann, Darden	Stuart Gilson, Harvard	Jean McTighe, Fleet Boston
Dana Clyman, Darden	John Glynn, Darden	Charles Meiburg, Darden
Trienet Coggeshall, Darden	Les Grayson, Darden	Barbara Millar, Darden
Dan Coleman, Fleet Boston	Benton Gup, Alabama	Michael Moffett, Thunderbird
John Colley, Darden	Joe Harder, Darden	Charles Moyer, Wake Forest
Bob Conroy, Darden	C.V. Harquail, Darden	James T. Murphy, Tulane
Lorri Cooper, Darden	Bob Harris, Darden	Chris Muscarella, Penn State
Martin Davidson, Darden	Mark Haskins, Darden	

Dan Newton, Darden	Mark Reisler, Darden	Rick Swasey, Northeastern
Ben Nunnally, UNC-Charlotte	Lee Remmers, INSEAD	Bob Taggart, Boston
Elizabeth O'Halloran, Darden	Kristian Rydqvist, BI Norway	Elizabeth Teisberg, Darden
Robert Parrino, UT-Austin	James Rubin, Darden	Max Torres, IESE
Mark Parry, Darden	Craig Ruff, AIMR	Katherine Updike, Excelsior
Marie Payne, Darden	Bob Sack, Darden	Bob Vandell, Darden
Gary Peters, Darden	Xavier Santoma, IESE	Nick Varaiya, UC San Diego
Larry Pettit, UVA-McIntire	Kris Seale, Darden	S. Venkataraman, Darden
Phil Pfeifer, Darden	Katrina Sherrerd, AIMR	Theo Vermaelen, INSEAD
Tom Piper, Harvard	Norman Siegel, Darden	Claude Viallet, INSEAD
Dennis Proffitt, Virginia	Betty Simkins, Oklahoma	Tiha von Ghyczy, Darden
Lou Rader, Darden	Randy Smith, Darden	Ingo Walter, NYU
Ahmad Rahnema, IESE	Ray Smith, Darden	Carol Weber, Darden
Latha Ramchand, U.Houston	Ted Snyder, Chicago	Jack Weber, Darden
Kamalini Ramdas, Darden	Kirsten Spector, Fleet Boston	Pat Werhane, Darden
Jude Reagan, Virginia	Robert Spekman, Darden	June West, Darden
Henry B. Reiling, Harvard	Betty Sprouse, Darden	Ulrich Wiechmann, UWINC
Jud Reis, Darden	Anant Sundaram, Thunderbird	Marc Zenner, UNC-Chapel Hill

Whatever these acquaintances have endured in the form of my questions, speculations, opinions, and writings, my wife, Barbara McTigue Bruner, and two sons, Jonathan and Alexander, have endured the most on behalf of case writing and case teaching. Development of this book would not have been possible without their fond patience.

All these acknowledgments notwithstanding, the responsibility is mine for any shortcomings remaining in this book. I welcome suggestions for its enhancement. Please let me know of your experience with the book and/or as a case teacher.

Robert F. Bruner
Distinguished Professor of Business Administration and
Executive Director of the Batten Institute
Darden Graduate School of Business
University of Virginia
Post Office Box 6550
Charlottesville, Virginia 22906
Email: brunerr@virginia.edu
Web site: http://faculty.darden.edu/brunerb/

Contents

Contents -- continued

Chapter 1
Introduction

Discussion-based teaching grows knowledge and wisdom in students through *dialogue*. Because of its focus on give-and-take, this method of teaching is often called *active learning*. It appears in numerous forms around the world: in one-on-one tutorials at English universities, in dialectical instruction in a number of the world's religions, in small university reading seminars, and in the discussion of cases in professional fields such as business, law, and medicine. The dialectical nature of this teaching approach is its most distinctive feature in comparison to the lecture-based teaching method. The skeletal frame of a discussion is a series of questions, usually posed by the instructor, sometimes by the student. All knowledge starts with a question, as Neil Postman and Charles Weingartner have said. Built onto the frame are facts, inferences, and most importantly, judgments. The master builder is the teacher who conceives a vision of the structure, and seeks to draw the students into completing it with him or her. This is achieved through careful management of content and process. Like a nineteenth-century American barn raising,[5] the joint work of teacher and students bonds disparate contributors into a community. Often the resulting structure is beautiful not only for the end result, but for the *way* it was achieved. However, there is no guarantee that discussion-based teaching will achieve such a result.[6]

The lecture method is much more controlled. The teacher is in charge. His or her main task is to manage content, which is a series of declarations. The role of the teacher is to *profess*. The job of the students is to take notes. Students come and go from one class meeting to the next with no particular interaction. The end result is the transfer of knowledge. If discussion-based teaching is like a barn-raising, lecture-based teaching is like mass-production. This method is justifiably called passive learning.

---

[5] The metaphor of barn raising as applied to discussion-method teaching was nicely explored by Don McCormick and Michael Kahn in "Barn Raising: Collaborative Group Process in Seminars," *EXCHANGE: The Organizational Behavior Teaching Journal*, Vol. VII, No. 4, pgs. 16-20.

[6] Though I have a strong bias in favor of the discussion method, it may not always be the best approach. Constraints of time and space, or a focus on transmitting information rather than building judgment, might impel one to lecture. A colleague wrote, "I started out my career teaching a course with 300 undergraduates using the discussion method. I had to shift to full lecture because the students could not hear each other, and few could see what I wrote on the board." In such settings, a lecture approach might actually be more student centered than discussions.

To shift from passive to active learning is a big stretch for students. I recall vividly my introduction to serious active learning. As an undergraduate, I had had a very good educational experience, mostly as a passive learner. I was unprepared therefore for my encounter with active learning in graduate school. In September 1972, I enrolled as an MBA student at Harvard Business School. The first class meeting of the program was to discuss a case about the company which made Butcher's Wax, used for polishing wood floors. The course was Marketing. I walked into an amphitheatre that seated about 90. Though I had read the case several times, I had been a liberal arts major, and was basically clueless about the issues. Just at the stroke of the hour, the instructor strode into the well of the amphitheatre, laid his notes on the desk, introduced himself, turned to a student in the front row, and said, "Mr. X, what are the issues in this case, and what do you recommend?" I thought I could smell ozone in the air, as if lightning had just struck. I looked around: eyes were widening; bodies were leaning in toward the well, poised on the edge of their seats. Mr. X nervously shuffled some papers, recited a few facts from the case, and began to sit back in his seat as if pleading for release. "But what do these facts mean?" erupted the instructor. Mr. X sat upright again and tentatively poked at an inconsistency within the company's marketing strategy. "Is this a problem for anyone?" Yes, probably so, since the company was spending a lot of money on marketing. The instructor paused and looked around. Slowly a dozen or more hands went up and he proceeded to widen the circle of discussion. The chalkboard began to fill up with lists of issues, drivers of outcomes, and diagrams about the relationship between the company, its retailers, and the consumer. This served to confirm that the data given in the case study were incomplete (we needed to know much more) and somewhat inconsistent (how could two sources of data disagree?) The classroom environment was mildly jarring. The exploration was not particularly linear. Students disagreed with one another. The professor simply asked questions and offered no guidance to confirm much of anything—though through body language, voice, and tempo of his questions one had a sense of guidance. Just as chaos seemed ready to take over, the germ of closure sprouted: a course of action that might get the company back on track. Then all too soon, the class period ended. I walked out of the classroom exhilarated, electrified, sure that I didn't know much, but also sure that I wanted to know a great deal more. I felt somewhat intimidated by the work that lay ahead, but also felt emboldened by seeing analysis and decision-making in the midst of uncertainty. That class marked for me a paradigm shift from passive to active learning. I can say that for my two years in Harvard's MBA program, I taught myself more intensely than ever before.

Starting to teach by the discussion method can require an equally large paradigm shift for instructors. This book surveys the scope and nature of this shift. But the core of becoming an effective discussion leader entails implementing a *student-centered attitude*.

It is true that there are many other drivers of teaching effectiveness: motivated students, good teaching materials, appropriate classrooms, etc.—I will speak to these kinds of drivers in this book, and do not discount their influence. But in this book, I want to shift the spotlight onto the instructor who must see the learning enterprise as the student sees it. This attitude drives good course design, selection of teaching materials, preparation of a teaching plan, arrangement of the classroom, learning about the students, response to challenges, grading and evaluation, receiving feedback, teaching other teachers—in short everything about teaching by the discussion method. Though having a student-centered attitude is no guarantee of success, I believe that absence of that attitude greatly increases the probability of failure.

The case study as a platform for discussion

In this volume, I use "discussion method" and "case method" interchangeably even though the case study is just one type of teaching material, and the case discussion is just one format that the discussion leader might choose. While the case method has its strongest roots in some U.S. business schools, I believe its teaching insights are relevant to all discussion leaders. To use the phrases interchangeably is to honor the catholicity of discussion leadership ideas, rather than to exclude other discussion materials or formats.

A case study is a summary of a problem situation that invites the student to recommend action based on analysis. It is teaching material, not a journalistic or historical record. The writer of case studies seeks to create a learning experience for students by re-creating the problem setting as decision-makers saw it at the time. A case study cannot be encyclopedic; it is necessarily an abstraction of reality that focuses on relevant considerations. Often with hindsight years after the date of the case, the instructor knows how wrong the decision-makers were at the time. Strong as the case writer's temptation may be to "set the record straight" a good case will throw students into the same setting as prevailed historically to let *them* wrestle with the same dilemmas, and perhaps even err—all for the purpose of helping students learn to avoid a similar mistake in professional life.

Why teach with the discussion method?

Successful discussion teachers must find meaning in the method. It is not sufficient to master the "how" of case teaching; one also needs to have a "why." Here are my whys:

1. **The discussion method is effective.** One learns best that which one teaches oneself. True learning is a process of self-discovery, as opposed to passive absorption of what others say. Student ownership and active engagement with the case problem are the keys to the effectiveness of this method. Some would argue that sheer technical material is best taught by lecture. The case method is at its best when the problem is uncertain and yet requires a decision. But I think it would be possible to have an effective discussion of any technical proposition (such as "water boils at 100 degrees Celsius"). To the extent that one uses case studies about real-life situations, the discussion material becomes more compelling to the student, and the learning deepens.

2. **The discussion method builds the capacity for critical thinking.** Instructors model skills of questioning. Discussions exercise skills of debate and challenge. The case method engages students in this process of exposure. We want professionals who are capable of thinking critically.

3. **The discussion method exercises judgment and action-taking.** If the goal of professional education is to enhance the effectiveness of decision-makers, then it is important to exercise students in the practicalities of analysis and decision-making. The best way to do this is to demand that recommendations always accompany analyses.

4. **The discussion classroom models a learning environment.** Through this, the student can learn how to achieve trust, respect, risk-taking, high quality of debate, and tough-mindedness in other professional settings. While much has been said about the "learning organization" in recent years, companies continue to grope slowly toward that goal. Whatever it finally emerges to be, a culture of high-quality dialogue will probably be at its core. The lecture-hall is a model of one-way information flow from the Master to the novice, and is not an example of the kind of give-and-take that one observes in the best organizations. John McArthur, Emeritus Dean of Harvard Business School, has said, "How we teach is what we teach."

5. **The discussion method models the process of inductive learning-from-experience that adults will employ throughout their lives.** Thus, the method prepares the student for life-long learning and for being a useful participant in a learning organization. As Walter Wriston said, "Good judgment comes from experience. Experience comes from bad judgment."

6. **The teacher learns too.** Because of the interactivity of this method, the teacher can encounter fresh perspectives on old problems, or test classic solutions to new problems. As Charles I. Gragg wrote years ago, "Not all the teaching should be

done by the teacher. Not all the learning should be done by the student."[7] Professor Robert Higgins wrote that

> *Two experiences relatively early in my career convinced me of the virtues of case method instruction; one was personal the other professional. The personal experience occurred in the middle of a lecture I was giving to undergraduates on discounted cash flow techniques when I realized that I was simultaneously lecturing and daydreaming. I had simply turned on the prerecorded lecture tape and was planning my afternoon's activities while the tape droned on. The thought immediately occurred, "Can I continue to give this lecture for another 30 years and retain my sanity, to say nothing of my enthusiasm?" Cases are a way to cover well-trodden ground in fresh ways. My professional experience involved one of the regular articles appearing in Business Week some years ago lamenting the deplorable quality of instruction in American business schools. It quoted a professor at a well-known university who asked why he should devote a lot of time to his lectures when the topic was invariably presented more elegantly and effectively in the textbook. I had to agree. Trapping fifty students in a darkened room and talking to the tops of their heads while they scribble notes can't be the most productive use of time--especially when the textbook says it better.[8]*

7. **The discussion method is fun.** It motivates students and energizes the instructor. Direct debate over practical problems stimulates student effort.

Overview of the book

This book is divided into six sections, each with its own introduction.

- Part 1 presents three case studies in case teaching. These afford a chance to engage the book as a learner and decision-maker yourself. My commentaries on these cases are given in Part 6.

---

[7] Gragg, C.I., "Because Wisdom Can't Be Told," in *The Case Method at the Harvard Business School*, ed., M.P. McNair with Anita C. Hersum, New York: McGraw-Hill, 1954. Available as reprint from HBS Publishing, Boston, MA, case number 9-451-005.

[8] Quoted from http://papers.ssrn.com/sol3/papers.cfm?abstract_id=148009.

- Part 2 argues that excellent teachers have an ideology or *view* about teaching that guides every choice they make.

- Part 3 addresses some practices for building strong discussion leadership.

- Part 4 addresses the *design* of the learning experience.

- Part 5 deals with frequent challenges, usually in the form of objections, which the teacher will likely confront. Give some attention in this section not only to the specifics, but also to an underlying perspective that can help guide you in unexpected circumstances.

- Part 6 considers how the teacher can solidify personal learning about discussion leadership. The aim of this final section is to stimulate further reflection.

How to approach the task of learning to lead discussions

> *You can approach the act of writing with nervousness, excitement, hopefulness, or even despair…Come to it any way but lightly. Let me say it again, you must not come lightly to the blank page.*
>
> --Stephen King[9]

Come to it any way but lightly. King's advice to writers is arresting. No gentle coaching here; no happy talk; but fundamentally sound advice for the professional pursuit of anything, especially teaching. We all recall stereotypes of teachers who *do* take it lightly: the gifted amateur, or the person who would really rather be doing something else and uses teaching as a filler. King's advice is that one should start by getting serious: don't come lightly.

Courage and passion fuel good teaching. There is more to the story than that, but as a point of departure, one must boldly summon the right attitude to become an excellent teacher and discussion leader. Surely, some will argue that one must be well trained in one's subject. Others will say that good teachers require good facilities, small classes, and eager students. Yet others aver that technique and mastery of process matter. In fact, these and other influences do matter; but their impact depends ultimately on the desire and will to teach better. To this I would add that passion carries one on to full mastery. If you want to learn to lead discussions very well, do not stint on care and attention, time and preparation, and fearless self-examination. With those qualities in hand, this book can help you get started.

---

[9] Stephen King, *On Writing*, New York: Scribner, 2000, pages 106-107.

Part 1
Three Mini-Cases On Teaching
By The Discussion Method

Overview

To stimulate your own learning about the discussion method of teaching, take some time to study the following three "mini-cases" about discussion leadership. A maxim of this method is that "one learns best that which one teaches oneself." Accordingly, it is appropriate to give you the opportunity to engage personally the kinds of problems addressed here. In that spirit, to get the most out of the examples consider doing the following:

- Study each case before moving on to the next.

- Read each case quickly, to get the gist of the problem, then read it again, more slowly, marking important facts and details that might influence your thinking.

- On a separate sheet of paper, make some notes about the problem, and actions that you would suggest.

- Tuck your notes away, and read Chapters 5 through 33 of this book. Look again at your notes, and make any more comments in them that you believe may be justified.

- Study Chapters 34-36, which contain my commentaries on the three cases— these are not the "right solution" in any sense, though you are bound to notice some similarities among the commentaries and my discussion in other chapters.

- Reflect: re-read your notes. Compare them to my commentaries. Talk about the cases with a friend. Think about variations on the themes; exceptions; rules or "oughts" you might offer to a novice. Revisit them again after you teach your next course. Consider how your thinking might have changed.

Chapter 2
Henry Domhoff

Henry Domhoff shuffled the teaching notes on his desk into a file folder, put on his jacket, and strode out of his office toward the classroom. He felt a mixture of fear and buoyancy: this was the first day of his MBA course on Law, Governance, and Corporate Strategy (LGCS) at Excelsior University. He had taught the course twice before (with middling teaching evaluations from students), and was now in his third year at Excelsior. He and the Dean would discuss his teaching evaluations and the renewal of his teaching contract in a few months. The course was a capstone for MBA students at Excelsior, taught by the case method. It was meant to mix practice and theory, to challenge the students, and exercise skills acquired earlier. The students would graduate in three months. Many of them had some work experience in investment banking. Most sought to go to Wall Street upon graduation.

His goals for this first class were to introduce the course, highlight specific requirements, and then launch into the discussion of a case study that would raise a number of themes to be addressed throughout the course. Henry sought to use this first class to establish some norms for the course regarding active participation, preparation, and cold-calling.

Henry arrived at class two minutes before the start, hung up his jacket, spread out his teaching notes, and turned to face the students. About 40 of the 55 enrolled students were in their seats. A few more students walked in as the official starting time arrived. He noted that the students had the option to drop the course after a couple of class meetings and that he often lost a few more students. Clearing his throat, he called the class to order. "I'm Henry Domhoff, and this is LGCS. The course syllabus covers details about the course, but I would like to mention some highlights…" Henry followed with 15 minutes of discussion about course objectives, the outline of topics, the use of cases, classes, and course norms. A few more students walked in during this discussion. As the minutes ticked by, the students seemed to grow restless or bored. But Henry soldiered on through the details. Finally, he reached the end, and just before beginning the case discussion with a cold-call, he asked for questions. Silence ensued. Then a student asked, "What relevance does this course have to investment banking?" Henry stammered something about concepts that would be generally useful. But before he could complete the thought, another student asked, "What is your practical experience? I mean, have you done any deals?" Henry felt himself blushing, for he had worked during his brief career only in academia. Then a voice from the back, speaking quietly enough that may have not been meant for his ears said, "Yeah, if you're so smart, why aren't you rich?" After a few nervous chuckles in the room, the students grew absolutely still. Henry was speechless as if sustaining a blow to the solar plexus. His first thought was, "This isn't starting the way I wanted."

Assignment to the reader:

1. What is (are) the problem(s) here?

2. What should Henry Domhoff do right away? In the near term? In the longer term, before he teaches the course the next time?

Chapter 3
Elizabeth Kent

Professor Elizabeth Kent found herself getting angry. An hour had passed in her 90-minute class, and the discussion was *not* following her lead. As she stood at the front of the classroom, she judged that the past hour had been a waste of time. It was true that the students seemed prepared and had plenty to say. But what they wanted to discuss was sharply different from what *she* had carefully planned for the session. The course was on a tight schedule and did not permit her to extend the discussion to the next meeting.

Elizabeth was a popular instructor at Acme University, teaching an over-enrolled course on Advanced Corporate Finance to MBA candidates. She set high standards for the students who, in turn, responded with hard work and ready preparation. The case for the day concerned the valuation of an investment in a leveraged buyout. Though the calculations were dense, she believed the students knew the drill. She wanted to get past the basic valuation exercise and into some higher ideas about the creation of value through the aggressive use of debt tax shields and creative deal design. She had published several papers on leveraged buyouts (LBOs) and had quite a lot to say to the students on the subject.

Elizabeth's key to teaching success, she felt, was her clarity about teaching goals each day. She framed her teaching plan to arrive at a closing mini-lecture of about five slides that would deliver closure on each case discussion, summarize some research, and offer her own views. Today she indulged herself by preparing eight slides and planned to give her remarks in the closing 20 minutes of the class. With 30 minutes now remaining, she needed to get the numerical work done in only ten more minutes.

The class had begun with her cold-call on a reasonably competent student. She asked him to frame the terms of the deal and the analysis that would be necessary to decide on whether to invest. Seconds into the class, the student derailed her teaching plan by launching a lengthy monologue about managerial conflicts of interest in LBO transactions. Other students energetically picked up the theme, debating the pros and cons of conflicts, illustrating them from their own work experience, and referring to principles in law, economics, and philosophy. The discussion assumed a life of its own.

Twice Elizabeth tried to get the discussion back on track. At one point, she interrupted a student and asked, "Well, how do you know that the conflict is worth worrying about unless you run some numbers?" The student responded by quoting his final valuation results that seemed to prove the existence of a conflict. Other valuation results bubbled up, unsolicited. Predictably, these valuation estimates covered such a wide range that one student blurted, "This deal is worth whatever you want it to be!" This prompted several comments about manipulation of financial forecasts and the reasonableness of the firm's strategic assumptions. None of this accomplished Elizabeth's goal of specifically estimating the value of debt tax shields in the deal.

Her second intervention occurred just a few minutes previously. Students had been debating whether LBO boutiques were a destabilizing force in the capital markets, an assertion that sounded pretty dubious to her. So she said, "Couldn't you view the boutiques as entrepreneurs who use a specific skill and set of network relationships to turn around aging firms? Isn't that good?" Well, this merely took the discussion further afield from her plan. She had stepped into her own trap.

Now, with 30 minutes left to go, she contemplated simply stopping the discussion cold and marching the students rapidly through a calculation of the numbers she wanted to obtain. And yet she hesitated...

Assignment to the reader:

1. What is (are) the problem(s) here?

2. What should Elizabeth Kent do right away? In the near term? In the longer term, before she teaches the course the next time?

Chapter 4
Eduardo Mendez

Eduardo Mendez slumped in his office chair with a mixture of fatigue and despair, even though the day was only half-finished. He would return to the classroom in two hours to teach the afternoon section of undergraduate-level introductory marketing. Right now, it seemed that something was going wrong in his course. He wondered what needed fixing, and how. Or whether. To change anything in mid-semester would be awkward.

His sense that things were not right was driven by a number of small facts and episodes:

- "So what's the right answer?" was a question he heard regularly from students, usually ten or so who came up to see him after each class. But occasionally he heard it during class. Eduardo gave very direct answers—usually his personal views—and sometimes distributed copies of his personal notes to make sure that students got the analytic points. He knew that in professional practice, none of the problems had strictly "right" answers. Moreover, the relentless request for "right" answers from students was, if anything, increasing during the semester. Wouldn't they ever be satisfied?

- The class discussions were routinely flat. There was little energy and no sense of humor in the classroom. The rate of participation was low—typically only 15 percent of the students offered comments or questions. Eduardo had chosen the case studies because they were classics—he had used them for years and had studied some of them as a student himself. The cases linked to phenomena in the real world. And many students had work experience related to the fields or problems in the case studies. Nevertheless, some of the students seemed tentative and uncertain—for this reason he almost never cold-called students in class. Other students were frankly coasting in their work effort. Students knew that 50 percent of their course grade would depend on class participation. Eduardo wondered how high he would need to raise the percentage in order to stimulate good discussion.

- 40 percent of the students earned unsatisfactory grades on the latest quiz. What surprised Eduardo was the fact that the quiz was based on a standard type of problem that had been repeated in three classes, estimating the firm's cost of capital. The quiz simply *reversed* the problem, asserting the solution, and asking students to solve for the assumptions that might be consistent with the solution. This appeared to confound a number of students. A couple of students had shown up at his office, angry and confrontational. He re-read their quizzes on the spot, and decided to add some points here and there, which raised their quiz grades a notch. Now word seemed to have gotten around. At his office hours, students stood in line outside his door to plead for a higher grade.

- An anonymous note, slipped under the door of his office, said that solutions to many of the case problems in his course were on the website of a large national college fraternity and that students were consulting these solutions in preparing for class. Eduardo confirmed the existence of these solutions and noted that some of these "solutions" contained the same errors that had cropped up in class. World University had a student Honor Code that proscribed cheating and plagiarism, though it was weakly enforced. In the faculty lounge, instructors openly scoffed at the suggestion that students weren't trying to cheat. No question had ever been raised regarding the potential honor violation if a student's preparation for class discussion weren't original.

- The teaching wasn't as much fun this semester as it used to be. He remembered discussions at another school that were animated, rich, and surprising. He learned something from each class. Now, it felt like he was going through the motions, and that he had to do all the pushing to make progress each day. His solution had been to become very directive in leading the discussions. But it seemed that the more directive he became, the more directive he *needed* to become. He felt tired. At this rate, he would barely make it to the end of the term. He took great confidence in knowing the cases so well that he would not have to invest much time in daily class preparation. Thus, even if he didn't have the energy, he wouldn't make a fool of himself.

World University had 25,000 students and was located in a large metropolitan area. Eduardo had a class roster from the Registrar, but did not have a clear idea of the backgrounds of his students. He believed that many of them were commuters who showed up at school solely to attend class. Most of the courses at World University were conducted on the lecture method and typically featured hundreds of students. Eduardo's class of 65 was arrayed in the usual fashion: rows of students facing front at movable tables, running in series to the back of the room. Students rarely met with each other outside of the classroom, typical of most courses at World University. Eduardo's course syllabus was terse, simply listing course requirements, meeting dates, and case assignments.

Eduardo, 32 years old and single, had taught at World University for three years. He occasionally had lunch with colleagues, when he could find them. Faculty and area meetings were rarely held, reflecting the reality that, like the students, the faculty tended to be commuters. Apart from office hours at the university, Eduardo tended to work at his apartment or at a corporation downtown for which he consulted part-time.

The memory of earlier teaching successes appealed to Eduardo. He wanted to turn the situation around. But he wasn't sure what to do, or for that matter, what was going wrong. Who was responsible for the deteriorating situation? What was the cause? Was there a "magic bullet" that would solve all the problems? What should he do starting this afternoon?

Assignment to the reader:

1. What is (are) the problem(s) here?
2. What should Eduardo Mendez do right away? In the near term? In the longer term, before he teaches the course the next time?

Part 2
Core Values

Overview

High-performing organizations are different from organizations that perform at the average. [11] Some are endowed with extraordinary resources (such as money or talent); a few have a strong and visionary leader; some others have a big idea that proved lucky at the right time. But common to them all tend to be strong internal commitments to a set of core values that knit together the "how," "what," and "why" of their activities. Many successful educational institutions have strong values regarding research. But what about regarding discussion leadership? The environment of culture and values has an enormous influence on the effectiveness of the discussion leader. Several core values can help him or her succeed.

The chapters in Part 2 survey some of the dimensions along which institutions and groups of instructors might orient their own cultures to promote excellent teaching. The list, not exhaustive, considers the following:

- **Ask often, tell seldom.** The example of Socrates explored in Chapter 5 illuminates some key aspects of the role of the instructor in the discussion-method classroom: to ask questions, to frame questions in a way that reaches both content and process objectives, to engage the student disarmingly. Strong discussion cultures empower the teacher to ask often and tell seldom.

- **Begin one's teaching and course design from the perspective of *the student*.** This is the essence of what it means to be student-centered. Chapter 6 describes what it means to think like a learner, and how one can "know" the student.

- **Exercise students' judgment because it builds wisdom.** Judgment in the form of decision-making is especially relevant in professional training. It is not enough to conclude that a patient is unconscious. One must decide *what to do next*. Chapter 7 explores what it means to be decision-focused and action-oriented.

---

[11] For example, see the study by James C. Collins and Jerry I. Porras, *Built to Last*, New York: Harper-Collins, 1997.

- **Research helps renewal.** Discussion leadership and research should not be mutually exclusive activities. They are complements. Research is vital for the renewal of teachers. Chapter 8 considers how research renews teachers and courses.

- **A key task of the teacher is to help students "make meaning."** The teacher's views are important. But a learning environment must be created that permits students to test their views

Some additional core values are suggested in later parts. But these initial five suggest the outlines of a discussion-based teaching culture within educational organizations.

Chapter 5
Socrates' Legacy:
The Primacy of *Asking*

The core of discussion leadership is the framing of questions that nudge students toward their own discovery of insights. Values associated with questioning are evident in the work of one of its earliest practitioners, Socrates. This philosopher and teacher lived from 469 to 399 B.C. in Athens. He wrote nothing. Rather like estimating the height of a distant mountain with instruments, we make the measure of Socrates through the possibly imperfect filters of others. Fortunately for the exploration in this book, there is little dispute about *how* Socrates taught. His legacy to the profession of teaching is twofold: he structured the educational experience as a *dialogue*, and modeled the discussion leader as a *participant* in the search for knowledge, rather than an expert who knew it all. He said that his greatest personal contribution was that "I taught men to question."

Among Socrates' contributions to philosophy was to suggest the importance of universal definitions as the basis for judgment. For instance, though there may be many sizes and shapes of birds, there are common characteristics that identify a creature as a bird. These characteristics form the universal definition. Socrates believed that inductive reasoning was the proper basis for discovering common characteristics. One reasons from specific facts to general propositions. This was a disinterested pursuit of truth through analysis. He conversed with students to draw out their views, and then examined the views critically. The conversational process became known as the *Socratic Method*. Through Socrates, we see dialogue as a cooperative search for truth and understanding. Plato records examples of these conversations in his dialogues, reconstructed scripts. Although the dialogues typically reached no complete closure, they advanced the student (and readers) toward insights of lasting importance.

The Socratic Method provides a helpful basis upon which to begin the identification of core teaching values for several reasons.

- The learning experience was based on questions, rather than statements. It was an experience in *active* learning.

- Socrates *engaged the students*. The student shared in the responsibility for the success of the discussion.

- Socrates' questions led somewhere—toward a consensus conclusion or universal definition. Socrates was a *leader* in the path and nature of his questioning.

- The point of the discussion was not to produce victory, as in a debate, but rather the growth of understanding.

- Socrates was very careful about assertions of his own—they are present in the way he framed questions.

- The process tended to expose ignorance—it was not necessarily comfortable for the participants.

- Socrates used the confident assertions of his students to challenge their own arguments. He drew out students' thinking by expressing ignorance (either actual or feigned). This famous tactic was called *Socratic Irony*. It modeled a radically different kind of educational leader, characterized by both expertise *and* humility.

John M. Cooper wrote:

> *Socrates was a totally new kind of Greek philosopher. He denied that he had discovered some new wisdom, indeed, that he possessed any wisdom at all, and he refused to hand anything down to anyone as his personal "truth," his claim to fame. All that he knew, humbly, was how to reason and reflect, how to improve himself and (if they would follow him in behaving the same way) help others to improve themselves, by doing his best to make his own moral, practical opinions, and his life itself, rest on appropriately tested and examined reasons—not on social authority or the say-so of esteemed poets (or philosophers) or custom or any other kind of intellectual laziness. At the same time, he made this self-improvement and the search for truth in which it consisted a common, joint effort, undertaken in discussion together with similarly committed other persons—even if it sometimes took on a rather combative aspect. The truth, if achieved, would be a truth attained by and for all who would take the trouble to think through on their own the steps leading to it: it could never be a personal "revelation" for which any individual could claim special credit.[12]*

---

[12] Quoted from the Introduction by John M. Cooper, in *Plato: Complete Works*, John M. Cooper, ed., Indianapolis: Hackett Publishing Co., 1997, page xix.

Meno by Plato

A good example of Socratic dialogue is given in *Meno* by Plato. This readily accessible[13] document is an important example of discussion leadership, and is "must reading" in the development of discussion leaders. The dialogue begins with Meno, a student of Socrates', asking "whether virtue is acquired by teaching or by practice." The ensuing exchange is illuminating, not only for what it tells us about virtue, but also about discussion leadership. Here are some highlights.

- In response to Meno's opening question, Socrates replies, "living as I do in this region of poverty, [I] am as poor as the rest of the world; and I confess with shame that I know literally nothing about virtue." This is a demonstration of Socrates' irony that disclaimed his expertise. When Meno scoffs at this, Socrates goes even further: "you may say further that I have never known of any one else who did, in my judgment" know anything about virtue. Then Socrates begins to question Meno, "By the gods, Meno, be generous, and tell me what *you* say that virtue is." Here, at the outset, we see the teacher drawing out the student, and starting the discussion *where the student is*.

- Illustrating the process of drawing out insights through questioning, Socrates teaches a slave boy the Pythagorean Theorem. The boy's answers are very simple, yet the resulting concept is sophisticated. Socrates asks Meno, "Do you observe that I am not teaching the boy anything, but only asking him questions?"

- The last third of *Meno* is devoted to Meno's question of whether virtue is acquired by teaching or acquired by nature. Socrates presses Meno and then Meno's friend, Anytus, to identify a teacher of virtue, anywhere. They fail to do so, suggesting that Socrates is about to argue that virtue is acquired by nature. But then the questions take a surprising tack as Socrates asks, "Then my dear friend, how can you know whether a thing is good or bad of which you are wholly ignorant?" With this, the discussion begins to build the argument that *knowledge* is the source of virtue, not direct teaching about virtue itself. Almost as an aside, Socrates says, "I am afraid, Meno, that you and I are not good for much…This I say, because I observe that in the previous discussion none of us remarked that right and good action is possible to man under other guidance than that of knowledge—and indeed if these be denied, there is no seeing how there can be any good men at all." Socrates and Meno consider the relative merits of true

---

[13] *Meno*, translated by Benjamin Howett, may be downloaded without charge from http://classics.mit.edu/Plato/meno.html.

knowledge versus mere opinion. They conclude that *both* right opinion and true knowledge are good sources of virtuous people.

- Socrates ends the dialogue abruptly without elegant summation and on the verge of a paradox that the reader must resolve: virtue is not acquired by nature, and yet there are no teachers of virtue—from where, then does the good person learn virtue? Connecting the dots, the reader is left to conclude that virtue is derived from knowledge, and that it is knowledge that is taught. Framing the closing as a paradox or set of questions for the student to resolve is a classic ending to a discussion (for more on this, see Chapter 27, "Giving Closure.")

Implications for today

The style of discussion leadership envisioned in this book is rather different from the directive questioning one will observe of Socrates in Plato's *Dialogues*—a colleague describes it as "frog-marching the students;" another says it is a lecture hidden in a dialogue. This may not be the perfect template for *modern* student-centeredness. Socrates himself is plainly the center; there is no obvious "partnership" with Meno or the slave boy; no joint agenda-setting. As Plato portrays the episode, Socrates seems to be grandstanding to the reader, rather than focusing all on Meno. Perhaps Socrates is the wrong Big Icon for a book on discussion leadership. Other Icons abound. Jesus truly began with a focus on the student, and employed questioning and parables in an extraordinary way. The conversations of Confucius reveal a less directive, more fluid teaching style. These and other great teachers suggest qualities that Socrates does not.

Still, Socrates warrants a position in the Pantheon of discussion leaders for at least two reasons:

- He models for us a teacher who *questions with intent.* He clearly knows where he is going. He has a vision in mind for the outcome of the educational enterprise. He gets there, not through assertion, but through questioning.

- His use of irony (which strikes some as false modesty and hidden arrogance) models for us nonetheless another important feature of discussion leaders: *detachment of the teacher from his or her own expertise.* To be visibly attached to what one knows—to be the expert—is insufficient to stimulate learning. Socrates chucked the pretense of expertise and sought to *enlist the student* directly through the student's own curiosity and participation in the discussion.

Instruction based on *asking* remains today a radical teaching model. And it raises interesting questions about the roles of student and teacher, and the interplay of ideas and action—these are addressed in the chapters that follow.

Chapter 6
Think Like a Learner,
Know the Learner

"When I was a boy of 14, my father was so ignorant I could hardly stand to have the old man around. But when I got to be 21, I was astonished at how much he had learned in 7 years."

-- Mark Twain[14]

Twain reminds us how different the world seems through younger eyes. Adopting the right perspective is crucial to helping the learner. Thinking like a teacher can get in the way of promoting student learning. Since the teacher's and learner's familiarity with the background and history of an idea differ, the learner is much slower to build context and grasp the concepts. Unless the teacher takes the perspective of the learner, the teacher might conclude the learner is stupid. To approach discussion leadership while thinking like a teacher is to start at a disadvantage.

Who is the learner?

The foundation to teaching success *is to think like a learner*. This "learner" could be the prototypical 20-year old occupant of a seat in a very large college lecture hall. Or he could be a 45-year old single parent who needs a few more degree credits of night school to get a pay raise. Or she could be an executive who has to figure out how the world is changing so that she can save her company. Or he could be a Ph.D. candidate in a small research seminar who is trying to become a teacher. Or she could be an unknown woman, barely knowledgeable of your language and culture, halfway around the world, linked by Internet or satellite to your class. Or he could be a consulting client who has retained you to help sort out a problem. In short, it is not sufficient to characterize this person as a stereotypical "student." More properly, this person is a *learner*. It is important to know who this person is. The first question all entertainers, preachers, writers, and teachers learn to ask is, "Who is the audience?"

---

[14] Mark Twain, "Bringing Up Father," *Reader's Digest*, 31 (Sept. 1937): 22.

To be student centered

Thinking like a learner is to take a student-centered point of view. This view has an august pedigree in teaching. John Dewey[15] articulated it. Alfred North Whitehead[16] and Carl Rogers[17] extended it. C. Roland Christensen[18] helped apply it. To be student centered has several important characteristics:

- One focuses on learning rather than on teaching.

- One starts teaching where the student is, rather than where one thinks the student ought to be.

- One holds that one learns best that which one teaches oneself. Learning occurs by the student and within the student.

- The professor is, at best, a guide. This is not to dismiss the responsibility of the teacher, but rather to recognize that the teacher must set up graduated experiences rather than end-point realizations.

- The learning process is necessarily a process of self-discovery for both student and teacher.

- The highest purpose of education is growth in wisdom, not merely the acquisition of information or knowledge.

- Wisdom cannot be told. This is the title of a famous essay by Charles Gragg[19].

To be student centered is hard. First, one must overcome one's own ego in approaching the teaching task. Second, the culture and peer expectations of teachers may militate against it. Third, it may be simpler to *tell* students than to set them up to work things out for themselves. And finally, learners themselves may get impatient: they may assert that

---

[15] Dewey, J., *How We Think*, Boston: D.C. Heath, 1933. See also Dewey, J., *Human Nature and Conduct*, New York: Random House, 1922, 1957.

[16] Whitehead, A.N., *The Aims of Education and Other Essays*, New York: Macmillan, 1929, 1957.

[17] Rogers, Carl, "Personal Thoughts on Teaching and Learning," pages 129-130 in Barnes, Christensen, and Hansen, 1994.

[18] Barnes, Louis B., C. Roland Christensen, and Abby J. Hansen, *Teaching and the Case Method*, Boston: Harvard Business School Press, 1994. See also C. Roland Christensen, David A. Garvin, and Ann Sweet (eds.) *Education for Judgment: The Artistry of Discussion Leadership*, Boston: Harvard Business School Press, 1991.

[19] Gragg, C.I., "Because Wisdom Can't Be Told," in *The Case Method at the Harvard Business School*, ed., M.P. McNair with Anita C. Hersum, New York: McGraw-Hill, 1954. Available as reprint from HBS Publishing, Boston, MA, case number 9-451-005.

they are the paying customers, and that they demand satisfaction—the satisfaction usually entails the instructor doing most of the work.

Being student centered will appear in virtually every aspect of the discussion method teacher's work. Consider the following eight areas (framed as diagnostic questions):

1. Have I **gathered relevant information** about the students I will teach?

2. Does my **course syllabus** start from an assessment of the students' mastery before the course, so that students get what *they*, not what I, need? (See Chapter 19.)

3. Does my **daily teaching plan** build on an understanding of how the students come into that class, and what will best prepare him/her for engaging the next class? (See Chapter 20.)

4. As I teach, do I **generally *ask*, rather than *tell*?** Do I frame my engagement with students as a series of questions, rather than statements? The importance of questioning appears repeatedly throughout this book. See, for instance, Chapter 4.

5. Do the teaching materials and plan require students to **do something "hands on"** in order to arrive at some closure for the material? Do they have to sort something out for themselves? Chapter 27 surveys the subtle but important issues in wrapping up a class. It may not be in the interest of student learning to spell all out for them at the end.

6. Do **I have some value** to add to the discovery process? How? Where? Do I intervene only after the students have engaged the material? Do I add guidance instead of answers?

7. Is the **feedback** I give on papers, exams, and class contribution oriented to where the student is, and calculated to help the student learn? The teacher-centered instructor will view feedback as a rather weary process of conveying data. The student centered instructor views feedback as a high-impact learning opportunity for students (and a possibly high-emotion event as well.)

8. Do I **slow down a little to listen better?** Listening well is an attribute of superior discussion method teachers. One listens with all one's faculties. But it is hard to "hear" if one is concentrating on saying something next that will impress the class, if one is in a hurry, or if there is a lot of background noise in one's life.

Being student-centered is no guarantee of success as a teacher. But the failure of student-centeredness is, in my experience, a very good predictor of failure. Be student-centered.

Think like a learner—this is a point emphasized by Soren Kierkegaard more than a century ago:

> ...if real success is to attend the effort to bring a man to a definite position, one must first of all take pains to find HIM where he is and begin there. This is the secret of the art of helping others.[20]

Know the learner

Perhaps the first requisite to thinking like the learner is to *know* the learner. Many instructors assume that because they have spent so many years in pursuit of an education, they have a very good idea of the learner. Yet times, conditions, and learning cultures change: what one learned about oneself as a learner in a different place, may not be so relevant to where you are today. Knowing the *object* of one's professional work is of such obvious virtue that it is surprising therefore how little university instructors know their students. The doctor is admonished to know the patient (and the disease); the lawyer, the witness (and the likely testimony); the clergyman, the parishioner; the actor, the audience; the marketer, the consumer, and so on. A fundamental admonition to teachers must be: *know the learner.*

Little in one's professional training prepares an instructor for this. Workload, personality, school culture, the physical layout of the school, and the always-present power asymmetry between student and teacher throw up numerous obstructions. Thus, the teacher often brings disadvantages to the task. How to know the student despite these drawbacks is an early challenge for the novice, and an enduring challenge for the experienced teacher.

The point of departure must be the number one rule for getting to know the student: *engage the students where they are.* To "engage" students is to participate in a dialogue or exchange of information—the instructor needs to know what to look, ask, and listen for. Where they are is obviously distinct from where *you* are—try to meet them afresh, absent of stereotypes. To meet them where they are is to gain a sense of their place on the learning path. Where they are can also imply *their* familiar location such as a classroom, hallway, cafeteria, etc.—get out of your faculty shell and reach out to understand them. Five devices can help the teacher engage the students where they are:

---

[20] Soren Kierkegaard, *The Journals,* 1864.

name cards, seating arrangements and charts, student information cards, small talk, and meetings in one's office.

Name cards or tents. The instructor should ask each student to place in front a card or piece of paper with first and last name clearly written. These help remind the instructor about the linkage between a name and a face. Even when the course has progressed to the point that you know most names, you should insist that the students continue to place their name cards in front of themselves. Otherwise it will become clear who you know, and who you do not.

Seating and seating charts. Seating has a huge influence on the ability of the teacher to know the students. Three tips are (a) arrange the seating to best advantage; (b) fix student seating; and (c) make a seating chart. Discussion thrives when students can talk to each other readily. Arranging students so that they easily face one another not only stimulates discussion but also helps acquaint the instructor with students who might otherwise be stuck at the back of the classroom. Most schools have desks and chairs arranged in rows. What one should strive for is a large "U"-shaped seating plan, with the open end facing the chalkboard. With large numbers of students it may be necessary to have concentric "U's"—but even so, the instructor can relate more easily to all students than with the typical row arrangement. Once seating is arranged, the instructor should ask the students to return to the same seat for the balance of the classes. The free spirits in class may complain until you emphasize that this will help you to get to know the students better, grade class contribution more accurately, and stimulate discussion (i.e., because students can anticipate where others will be in the classroom.)

Student information cards (a.k.a. "Face cards"). These are index cards that give a picture of the student, and a few relevant details, such as prior work experience, other university degrees, age, home town, marital status, and number of children. Some of this information may seem unnecessary until one realizes how differently one's students may enter your classroom. Suppose student A is a 38-year old single parent of a couple of children, has 15 years of work experience as a production supervisor, holds an MA in engineering and was born in Moscow. Student B is 21, single with no children, holds a BA in Art History, lives on campus, was born and raised a few miles away, and worked as a lifeguard for the past four summers. These two students will engage your course *very differently.* Anticipating the difference can forearm the instructor.

Most schools prepare student directories of some sort, often in book form. But having this information prepared in card form helps in two important tasks: record keeping and memorization. A colleague of mine walked into his first day of teaching at Darden by greeting the class and asking students to put their name cards away. Then he walked around the room—to all 100 students—and greeted each by first and last name. The students gave him a thunderous, standing ovation, at the successful completion of this prodigious and courageous[21] act. One may not have the time or random access memory capacity to learn all names and faces before the first class, but *a reasonable goal should be to know all the students by name soon after the start of the course.* Students appreciate recognition by name. It suggests a personal bond between instructor and student, and clearly shows that the instructor is making an effort to know them. This not only builds a sense of classroom community but also credibility in the classroom contribution grades that one calls. Donald C. Hambrick wrote,

> Students will attend to you if you attend to them. I try to learn all the students' names even in a class as large as 60, in the first three weeks, becoming able to address them by name without their name cards in the classroom and in the halls. This task is particularly essential because I grade class participation and can only do so credibly if it's clear I know who's who. When students do a particularly terrific job in class discussion—especially students who seem generally reluctant to talk—I try to grab them after class or put notes in their student folders saying what I liked so much about their contributions. I've also been known to communicate similarly with students who are a drag on class time.[22]

Having the information in face card format helps in two other respects. First, one can easily distribute cards to the students for verification of facts. Second, one can ask students to augment the information on their face cards with answers to several questions—it is important that the instructor tell students that their responses will be held in confidence:

- *Where are you from?* This simple question would seem to summon a simple answer, and in many cases it does. But a material fraction of students will tell an interesting story in response that often illuminates learning needs or opportunities.

---

[21] This is a highly effective means of differentiating oneself from one's colleagues, and not always appreciated among one's colleagues who may dismiss it as an attention-grabbing stunt. Also, the opportunities to make mistakes are legion. Pictures on the face cards may not be the most current representation of the student. Facial hair, hairstyles, eyeglasses, and body weight readily vary. Some names are difficult to pronounce. And the occasional error by the administrative staff has included switching photos, and reversing first and last names. One cannot simply rely on information from others. One's own discovery of the students is indispensable, as is a sense of humor.

[22] Donald C. Hambrick, "Teaching as Leading," in *Researchers Hooked on Teaching*, Rae Andre and Peter J. Frost eds., Thousand Oaks, CA: Sage Publications, pages 247-8.

- *Of what professional accomplishment are you proudest?* This can reveal at least three important clues about students. First, one may learn about pockets of expertise or life experience that may be relevant to the subject of the course, or to specific discussion sessions. Second, it may tell you something about the level of self-confidence and self-esteem of the student. Finally, some students may have no accomplishments to discuss—this, too, is an interesting revelation.

- *After I finish this program, I would like to get into_____.* This invites the student to discuss future plans, some of which may be relevant to forthcoming class discussions. Some students will express very clear plans; others will frankly admit cluelessness. These too are useful insights into the students.

- *So far, my experience at XXXX school has been_____.* This helps bring to your attention students who may be struggling. Some instructors will not ask this question, preferring not to bias one's thinking with impressions from the student. Others believe that self-reported information like this helps one prepare to help the student.

Daily notes. The most meaningful way to gain real insight into the learning progress and challenges of your students is to keep a record of class contribution. Specific tips about how to keep these notes are given in Chapter 28, "Grading Class Contribution." As we know from working with students, *writing down facts and concepts is an important learning technique.* Keeping daily notes about student progress is a simple expression of this truth. It is not so much what gets captured on paper that counts but rather the impression that is shaped in the instructor's mind. Notes help in the shaping process.

Small talk. Short, but frequent, conversations can do a great deal to help the instructor grasp the individual student, as well as the mood of the entire class. Be proactive in seeking to engage students in conversation. The typical instructor is introverted and loaded with work. The culture of the school may not encourage casual conversation. And the implied power of teacher over student may suppress candor. Nevertheless, many small bites of information are easy to digest and often contain enriching morsels not offered in other settings. Four tips are:

- **Arrive early to class.** Get there 10-15 minutes early. Turn on the lights; arrange the seating. Get chalk and/or test the projection system. Spread out your notes. Create a mental space for your class that is about to start. And then watch and listen as students arrive. Walk around the room; greet students where they are. Break the ice with simple conversation: school sports, the weather, the daily news. *Above all, pay attention to what you see and hear.* Look for patterns, and deviations between today's arrivals and those of previous classes. One could prepare a student for a "warm call" (in contrast to a "cold call") by telling him or her that you intend to invite that person to open the class discussion.

- **Stay after class.** Don't be in a hurry to leave. Students will often have questions arising from the class discussion. If you deal with them after class, you help the student resolve quickly any lingering confusion *and* you forestall future scheduled meetings in your office. Pay attention to the nature of the questions and who asks them. Watch the body language and mood of the students for clues about their engagement with class that day—or simply ask them how they are doing, how the work is going, what are their biggest concerns with the course.

- **Offer some easy informal access: listen and observe.** Get out of your office and into the social nexus of the school each week. This may mean going to regular morning coffee breaks or hanging around the cafeteria after lunch. These encounters—away from the classroom—offer ideal opportunities for small talk with students that can give you a fresh perspective on them and their engagement with your course.

- **Watch the school environment.** Go to student social events and listen. Read the student newspaper. Attend the student orientation at the start of each year. Sit in on other classes and listen.

Scheduled office meetings. Holding "office hours" or making specific appointments yields a richer opportunity to get to know the student. In a private setting, students may admit fears, anger, or confusion more readily than elsewhere. One often learns about other things in the school environment or student's life that impede learning. Office appointments are expensive in terms of the time one must set aside. To make it a really productive engagement, at the time of making the appointment I like to ask about the subject of the meeting and then to encourage the student to prepare questions, offer examples, on which we could focus our discussion. I encourage the student to review these issues with a study group member or friend, so that we can focus on the meatiest issues. On the principle of meeting students where they are, I often begin office meetings with "How is it going?" or "How can I help you?"

Conclusion

Think like a learner to become student centered. Invest in knowing the learner that you might better think like a learner. Knowing the learner is costly. Finding the right amount of investment will vary with experience, school culture, and attributes of students. But knowing the learner is indispensable for effective teaching.

Chapter 7
Decision Focus, Action Orientation

"Not to decide is to decide."
-- Harvey Cox

Turning analysis into actionable recommendations is a hallmark of the professional. After all, it is *decision-making* that creates action. And as Harvey Cox reminds us, deciding is inescapable. Preparation for professional life should exercise students' skills in drawing out action insights from analysis. An example of analysis without action is determining that a patient's temperature has risen to 100 degrees Fahrenheit, and then doing nothing about it. Analytic work is, by its nature, only descriptive. The role of the teacher must be to motivate students to extract the actionable insights. The verb, "educate," derives from a Greek verb meaning, "to draw out." A complete learning experience draws out the action insights from analysis.

Some typical objections and student-centered replies

Focusing one's teaching on student decision-making and action encounters four classic objections from teachers, administrators, and students themselves.

- **"The students can't do it; I have to do it for them."** Under this view, students are too immature, naïve, or unprepared to make decisions or offer action steps, so the teacher launches into a monologue about "Here's what I would do in this situation." All too often this view masks a teacher centered attitude (e.g., teacher can't stand to watch students fail; teacher knows best; teacher must remain in complete control; or that the teacher structured a problem too hard for the students at their stage of development.) And the remedy, ("Here's what I would do") usually fails to make much of a learning impact. The teacher can't promote student learning by making decisions and action recommendations for students. The vital role of the teacher is to present decision problems reasonably within the grasp of students, and then help them make meaning: emphasize the importance of decision-making and continually demand that students derive action recommendations from their analyses.

- **"The students don't like to make decisions and recommendations."** It puts students on the spot. Novices feel ill prepared to decide. They may feel uncomfortable with ambiguity and unaware that decision-making *generally* embraces ambiguity. While most students have an appetite for tools and concepts, they show an aversion for decisions and action. Asking for recommendations seems confrontational. The instructor who is anxious about winning friends and gaining decent teaching evaluations may feel like skirting decisions and recommendations.[23] But learning is rarely a comfortable exercise. The mark of the excellent instructor is to achieve the right balance between demands and capabilities of the student.

- **"The students are undisciplined. Their recommendations are a waste of time."** Whose time is wasted in practice decisions? Not the students. Students are in school to gain the mental discipline necessary for professional life. If the objective is to promote learning, take the time to let students make poor recommendations—if you respond thoughtfully, their recommendations will improve with practice.

- **"It is unrealistic to train young people to be decision-makers."** Thus do administrators, instructors, and job recruiters challenge professional schools for aiming too high. After all, they argue, aren't most entry-level jobs concerned with mundane problems such as research, analysis, and customer service? By training young people to make hard decisions, some say that schools create unrealistic expectations that employers will be unable to fulfill for years. The counterargument is that it is never too early to stimulate true growth. Furthermore, mere skills of analysis, research, and customer service, are easily obtained by most organizations. Survival and prosperity of organizations depend on qualities in much shorter supply: wisdom, planning, decision-making, and leadership of action programs—virtually every career today requires these attributes.

One builds skills of decision and action-taking through trial-and-error exercise. Ben Franklin wrote, "Failure is the best teacher, you learn the lesson first." To produce intelligent new professionals, we need to exercise and practice their skills before they begin to work.

---

[23] This is a canard, of course. Research rejects the hypothesis that easier courses get higher course evaluations.

How to be more action-oriented

The teacher can help students, in both case and lecture courses, to develop their decision orientation in the following kinds of ways:

1. At the **start of the course**, announce in the syllabus and orally that students must come prepared to identify business decisions embedded in the case or problems, and to make recommendations regarding the business decisions.

2. **Choose cases and teaching materials** that require meaningful decisions and debatable recommendations. Problems that pose a dilemma or choice between alternatives will offer rich opportunities for discussion. Alternatively, if the materials for the day are descriptive or purely analytic, the teacher should shape a decision problem around them. Problems for which the solutions are obvious or require little judgment may serve other instructional objectives but do not advance the capacity of students to decide.

3. **Offer homework questions** for each class that stimulate the decision-orientation. At the very least, ask students what they would recommend that the case protagonist do. What are the managerial implications of his or her analysis? Obviously, some classes may necessarily focus on identifying problems rather than finding solutions—but even in these, the instructor could invite students to hypothesize about the decision alternatives that may lie ahead.

4. **In each class, ask students** for their recommendations on the problem of the day. This is most easily accomplished by a directed question at the start of a discussion. Invite others to comment or expand on those recommendations. At the very end of the discussion, one can ask the student who opened the class to reflect on any changes in recommendations that he or she might make, based on insights that emerged during class.

5. **Encourage students to take a stand.** As Chapter 24 suggests, a stand means having a point of view about the problem, a recommendation, and an analysis to back up both of them. This may be asking a lot of people who are new to your field. Be careful not to belittle the efforts of novices to make practical recommendations. *Think like a learner.* Look for the seeds of good action ideas, and invite students to rethink less worthy elements.

6. Each day include in your **teaching plan questions** that emphasize decision and action. For example: "What do you recommend?" "What will you do?" "What will you say?" "When will you say it?" "To whom will you say it?" "How

might others react?" "What will you do if the reaction is adverse?" Asking "why" is a natural follow-up to any of these questions.

7. **Assign brief papers** that require students to write about their recommendations and decisions. In the hurly-burly of discussion, less confident or introverted students may hesitate to express their ideas orally. But given an opportunity to reflect, they may demonstrate previously unknown capacities.

8. **Test** for the capacity to make decisions and recommendations. In preparing written exams, many instructors pose discrete gradable questions. Why not add one or more questions that exercise the student's decision focus and action orientation?

Conclusion

Decision-laden classes have their problems, too. Requiring decisions on the basis of incomplete information and partial or flawed analysis can encourage hasty judgment: ready, fire, aim. We all laugh at Yogi Berra's advice: "When you come to a fork in the road, take it." But the polar opposite, the analysis paralysis of "ready, aim, aim, aim . . ." is equally pernicious. Most professional people commend decisiveness of any sort over indecision.

The world needs action-oriented professionals. Educational programs should prepare students for the requirements of practical life. The classroom is an important laboratory in which to practice extending analysis into recommendation and action. Be decision-focused and action-oriented in your teaching and your students will too.

Chapter 8
Ideas Have Consequences:
Why Research Matters for Excellent Teaching

Consider the job description that academia gives to new professors. It reads something like this: Your job includes two primary tasks. Task One will earn you an increased salary, will secure your professional mobility, will enhance the reputation of your employer, will result in invitations to attend interesting conferences nationally and internationally, and can be done on a flextime basis and at home. Task Two is unlikely to enhance your salary, save your tenure decision, or increase your professional mobility significantly, and may, if pursued with too much enthusiasm, undermine these. This task will tie you down to fixed hours at fixed locations to be determined, but increasingly, as the student body ages and you gain enough experience to teach in graduate and executive programs, it will include nights and weekends. Task Two may result in your infrequent attendance at conferences held at out-of- the-way locations. Your challenge, should you decide to accept it, is to do both of these tasks well and with enthusiasm.[24]

-- Rae Andre and Peter J. Frost

"What is going on here? A scandal, really. And drivel, mostly. Millions of dollars exchange hands every fall between anxious parents and the clerks in college bursar's offices so that young Jasons or Heathers may sit at the feet of 'scholars' who will teach them for a precious few weeks. But the real action in the university isn't teaching: it's the fight for preferment among faculty members, and the coin of the realm is published 'scholarship'—even of the most ersatz sort…'tedious, slippery…sectarian, humorless, pedantic and self-endeared'…[and] almost completely worthless."[25]

-- Philip Chalk

A teacher stretched between Task One and Task Two reads critiques like Chalk's and wonders whether pursuing research really *is* consistent with being student centered. Some critics of the academy advocate the abandonment of research for the single-minded

---

[24] Rae Andre and Peter J. Frost, "Introduction," *Researchers Hooked on Teaching* Thousand Oaks CA: Sage Publications, 1997, pages xi-xii.
[25] Philip Chalk, "From the College Reading Room: A look at what passes for scholarship these days," *Wall Street Journal*, January 25, 2002, page W15.

pursuit of teaching. These critics say that research is unreadable, that it has no relevance to realistic problems, that research bores students, that alumni and recruiters don't care whether students master research, and that scholarly ideas have had no impact on practical affairs. The critics often advocate a return to "basics," which means focusing most of the faculty time on teaching rather than research, on tools rather than concepts, and on practice rather than theory. It is not clear what problems these remedies are meant to solve, but if improving student wisdom and learning is their aim, the abandonment of research as a discipline in the teacher's life is the wrong way to go.

Why research matters

First, **curiosity and an attitude of discovery are vital** attributes of good teachers. It builds a teacher's passion and sense of engagement with a subject field—students can sense a teacher's personal engagement with a subject, which only increases the odds of animated classroom discussions (see Chapter 25 for more on how this happens.) Many researchers view teaching as an extension of their work of inquiry. In an excellent essay, Karl Weick relates that teaching for him is *learning in public*—that is, in the classroom.

> My teaching experience feels integrated because it doesn't involve teaching at all. Instead, it involves learning in public. By teaching, I mean transmitting knowledge and information in ways that help people acquire what has been prestructured. Teaching is about imparting information, direct showing, furnishing necessary knowledge, instructing, and realizing specific a priori intentions. Teaching resembles training rather than discovery. I understand learning to have a different character. Learning is about creating knowledge, structuring, punctuating information out of a stream of experience, imposing structures on experience, connecting, experimenting with language that captures novel nuances, and disorganizing in the service of restructuring. Learning relishes the multiple meanings that unsettle teaching. Learning complicates; teaching simplifies....Faced with the choice, I opt for learning.[26]

Second, there are strong parallels between the discovery process in research, and the discovery process of **finding an "aha"** in the student's mind. Science tells us that one can never really *prove* an idea; one can only disprove other ideas. By a process of elimination, one arrives at an explanation for phenomena that *survives* challenges. That doesn't mean the explanation is necessarily Truth but that it merely outlasts other

---

[26] Karl E. Weick, "Teaching as learning in public," *Researchers Hooked on Teaching*, Rae Andre and Peter J. Frost, eds., Thousand Oaks, CA: Sage Publications, 1997, page 286.

explanations—students need to understand this about received knowledge as the basis for their growth in wisdom. But to continue, student-centered learning follows a similar path by which *the student* struggles through false facts and explanations to find the "aha." Scientific research models for us the discovery process we hope to see in our students.

Third, don't discount the **value of academic debate**. Though the academy (like legislatures, corporations, and other large bodies) may move slowly to reject false ideas, the process is inexorable. The early Humanists taught us that holding ideas up to critical public examination and proving them in that arena is the only effective way to reveal Truth. Here too, the case method classroom mirrors the process of dissemination of ideas. Agnosticism or ignorance of concepts only puts our students at a disadvantage relative to those who understand the ongoing debates. Barbara Gutek wrote:

> [A]ny subject, even a controversial one, is amenable to research. In fact, research is especially important in controversial areas where opinions are typically strong and ideologically based and are often supported by firsthand experience or hearsay but not by research results. Research is what allows us to separate myth from fact, and it provides a solid basis for action.[27]

Fourth, research **promotes teachers' and students' capacities for critical thinking**. Professional development of teachers that focuses only on an accepted canon of ideas easily degrades into rote teaching. Does this promote the kind of professionalism that society needs? I don't think so. We need people who *think for themselves: critically, calmly, and compassionately.* Gutek wrote,

> Research findings play several important roles in teaching. First, they support the utility of the concepts and theories that are presented. Second, empirical research is important to help persuade people of reality. It can help them get out of a set frame....students do not often accept theories without research support. (Even then, they often prefer to stick with strongly held beliefs.) Third, they teach people to think critically about information presented to them and especially to question personal experience and anecdote as methods of learning.[28]

Fifth, research is **vital for establishing even the "basics"** to which teachers might return. Without the processes of research and peer-reviewed publication, the "basics" would be whatever bureaucrats or special interest groups say they should be. Ideas have

---

[27] Barbara Gutek., "Teaching and research: A puzzling dichotomy," in *Researchers Hooked on Teaching,* Rae Andre and Peter J. Frost, eds., Thousand Oaks, CA: Sage Publications, 1997, page 29.
[28] *Ibid.* page 31.

consequences[29] which, left unexamined, could do harm. A world without university research would become expensive to society. For instance, absent research in the social sciences, public policy makers would face a course of trial-and-error, of learning what works only by experience. As the advice columnist, Ann Landers, once wrote, "The trouble with using experience as a guide is that you get the grade first and the lesson later."

Sixth, research **refreshes the teachers**. It keeps them intellectually alive and alert to news and its implications. Students want keen instructors. Donald C. Hambrick wrote,

> [I]t keeps me fresh and energized. Without research, I would be stale. Teaching is great, and it can be a source of short-term energy, but it is essentially an emptying activity; replenishment must come from somewhere. I don't know whether evidence would bear me out, but I would guess that teacher burnout is far more prevalent and severe among professors without active research programs than for those who are significantly involved in original research.[30]

Nobel Laureate Richard P. Feynman said,

> The questions of students are often the source of new research…they *remind* me of a problem by asking questions in the neighborhood of that problem. It's not so easy to remind *yourself* of these things…I would *never* accept any position in which somebody has invented a happy situation for me where I don't have to teach. Never.

Seventh, teaching and research are similar in the sense that **they both address an audience**. To do research and get it published entails a set of skills that help develop one for the classroom. Rae Andre wrote:

> All writing and speaking is teaching. All teaching is influence. Teaching is the act of convincing an audience to consider a point of view (if not to agree with it) and to learn a certain set of facts and/or ideas. Teaching is the buzzword for influencing students. Research is the buzzword for influencing colleagues.[31]

---

[29] For more on this, see the classic work by Richard M. Weaver, *Ideas Have Consequences* Chicago: University of Chicago Press, 1948, 1984.

[30] Donald C. Hambrick, "Teaching as leading," in *Researchers Hooked on Teaching*, Rae Andre and Peter J. Frost, eds., Thousand Oaks, CA: Sage Publications, 1997, page 252.

[31] Rae Andre, "If it's Not Teaching and Research," in *Researchers Hooked on Teaching*, Rae Andre and Peter J. Frost, eds., Thousand Oaks, CA: Sage Publications page 48.

And eighth, an instructor's interest in research **exemplifies for students the attributes necessary to confront a world awash in research**, some of it good, much of it indifferent or bad. The key attribute here is the ability to think critically about questions, hypotheses, data, tests, and interpretation of results. To the outsider, such ruminations seem arcane. But when millions of dollars of investment value hang on an analysis, or the justice of a court decision hangs on questions of evidence, or a life hangs on a diagnosis of data, one sees vividly the virtue of thinking sensibly about research.

A profession of research *and* teaching

The solution is to integrate one's teaching and research activities, to be the whole professional. The way to do this is to *think like a learner.* In developing a course design, preparing to teach, actually teaching, and afterward reflecting on the experience, one should ask, "What can I learn from this teaching experience?" The adoption of a learning attitude unifies teaching and research. Consider some discrete ways in which research and teaching can be linked through a learning attitude:

1. **Seek teaching assignments** in your area of research interests.

2. **Experiment with teaching materials** with the discipline of a researcher. Why do some materials work, and others fail? Choose some new teaching material each year that stands a strong chance of telling you something new, about the subject, the students, and yourself.

3. Invite a colleague to **sit in**, and then discuss the content of the class afterward.

4. **Listen hard to the questions** of the students. All too often, we leap to deliver answers, without reflecting on the origins of students' questions and their implications. Some of my best research ideas have emerged from the questions of students.

5. To each class discussion, **aim to bring something extra** that draws upon your own work (a graph, some results, a derivation) and invite students to draw inferences from it, offer objections or counter-examples, etc. But be careful to stay student centered in the way you introduce such material.

6. **Co-teach** with a colleague whose research expertise complements or mirrors your own, or whose vision is contrary to yours.

7. **Drill down into a field of research.** This stage focuses on mapping the field, the players, and the issues. Rather like an American going to Britain and trying to make sense of professional cricket, one has to work hard to get the lay of the land.

Some of the barriers will be daunting: vocabulary, concepts, research methods, evidence, data, tests, and mathematics. But with surprisingly little effort you can make headway. Get some guidance for your discovery process; a good mentor can help a lot here.

  a. See what some textbooks have to say about the general issues and ideas in that field.

  b. Do a search of research articles, and read a cross-section of them. The Internet makes searches relatively easy. Many journals now have search engines on their websites

  c. Email or call some of the authors with questions you may have.

  d. Attend professional conferences in this research area. Gain a sense of the current debates in the field.

8. **Get a view**. Form your own opinion about the issues in the field. Be careful of the knee-jerk tendency to reject ideas that seem difficult or counterintuitive, and of the opposite knee-jerk tendency to accept views promoted by leading textbooks. Having a view means having a critical perspective on received wisdom.

In short, one must surely be his own best critic, but at the same time should use research as a foundation for great student-centered teaching.

Chapter 9
Helping Students "Make Meaning:"
Whose Views Matter? And How?

In the student-centered classroom, whose views rule? The point of scholarship is to have a critical view about the tools and concepts in one's field; faithfulness to oneself would seem to dictate that you should teach that view. But students have views as well, despite denials or strong reluctance to express them. They bring into the case discussion a stew of assumptions, past experiences, needs, values, deep reflections, attitudes, knee-jerk reactions and everything else one might list under the heading of a "view." Views inevitably invite difference. It is the difference in views that makes the case discussion method powerful as a learning technique. Where, in the student-centered learning experience, can (or should) the teacher's views appear? And how should the teacher manage the inevitable difference?

The dilemmas surrounding any answers to these questions are illuminated through two examples:

- Teacher A serves her role as a "traffic cop:" directing the flow of the cars and trucks on the street, oblivious to what is actually in them. She is the completely neutral discussion leader. She believes that each case teaches itself, and that therefore students must talk about what *they* want. For her, student centered teaching must strictly be a process of student discovery, of, by, and for the student. Student evaluations of her teaching beg for direction, and for her to suppress the volume of useless comments in the class. "I'm lost in this course," said one student. "It's a hodge-podge of discussion. Half the students are trying to get somewhere with their comments, but are heading in 20 different directions. The other half has no idea where they're heading but try to say *something* each day so that they don't fail on class participation."

- Teacher B is a "true believer" about theoretical underpinnings of his course, with strong views on one side of every debate in his field, and has strong opinions about the world outside. He intervenes frequently to make sure the discussion stays on a pre-determined track, to reach a pre-determined destination. Each of his classes ends with a mini-lecture to ensure that students understand his views. He says, "I like to tell 'em what I'm gonna tell 'em, then tell 'em, and then tell 'em what I told 'em." He clashes occasionally with students who appear to disagree with his views and leaves a trail of sullen students who feel they were slammed for disagreeing with him. Student evaluations call this instructor "directive," "serious," and "intimidating." One student said, "Getting a good grade in this course is a matter of guessing what [Teacher B] wants to hear, and giving it to him. Fortunately my fraternity brothers took his course last year, and told me what to say."

The first rule about "views"

The traffic cop makes chaos. The true believer invites ventriloquism. Both ignore one of the fundamental roles of the teacher, to help students *make their own meaning* about the subject matter of the course. The objectives of an education should be not only to impart information and views but also to prepare students for life-long learning, i.e., to prepare students to make their own meaning about things in the future, unguided by an instructor. The traffic cop assumes too much about the students; the true believer, too little.

The first rule for deciding how much of your own views to inject into the students' learning experience is to *be guided by the students' opportunity to make meaning, and a realistic assessment of their capacity for doing so.* To "make meaning" out of a fact, tool, or concept that one encounters is to understand it as part of a larger context, to know how to act on it, and to *own* it as something that is personally valuable—or if not valuable, then to own the critical judgment about why it is not. The challenge for the instructor is to shape the self-teaching effort.

- The *opportunity* is a function of the subject matter and teaching materials. One needs to be reasonable about setting goals for each day. The true believer will see a wide range of issues to cover in any one class—and will try to cover them all. The traffic cop won't set goals, trusting instead that students will find in a case discussion whatever they choose to find.

- The students' *capacity* for making meaning is driven by a host of developmental attributes (age, work experience, intelligence), cultural attributes (e.g., self-reliance versus reliance on the instructor), and environmental attributes (e.g. the time available for homework, the existence of study groups, etc.) The traffic cop places overwhelming faith in students' capacity; the true believer places little faith.

Plainly, the judgment required of an instructor is extremely challenging. But many of the chapters offered in this book lend a foundation for judging the students' opportunities and capacities for making meaning.

Why meaning making is an important element of effective discussion leadership

In the 1930s and 1940s, Adelbert Ames of Dartmouth College studied the nature of perception using optical illusions. His findings suggested that our grasp of "reality" is actually an image of true reality as filtered through the human nervous system. The filtering role of the nervous system means that perception is heavily influenced by our needs, past experience, and assumptions. Humans rely on their perceptions of reality, until the perceptions fail to be useful or helpful. Perception is largely a matter of the words available to the person—we *know* only in the words available to describe knowing. A perception is meaningful mainly for how it makes us *act*. Neil Postman and Charles Weingartner[32] constructed a theory of education as "meaning-making" upon these findings. They offered various insights into the task of learning, and what it means for a teacher to "think like a learner":

- "Reality" is not an absolute, but rather is what the student makes of it. Even relatively simple ideas will be filtered and shaped into different realities by different students. Filtering and shaping are driven by needs (e.g., for food or sleep), assumptions, and experience.

- Students are unlikely to change their perception of the world until it stops working for them in some way. Failure is an important part of the learning process, the process by which students give up faulty perceptions, and acquire workable perceptions. Thus, trial-and-error is vital; active learning is effective learning.

- Community of learning assists in the change process. Students bring to the learning enterprise their unique filters and perceptions. Seeing alternative points of view, discovered through discussion, assists in the acquisition of what works better.

- A perception is meaningful to the extent that one knows how to act upon it. Thus, *learning is a process of "making meaning" about the world.*

The notion that to learn is to "make meaning" is a different—and I think much more useful—metaphor for framing the teaching challenge. It goes much farther than the popular view that learning is the acquisition of information, for it ties learning to action.

---

[32] Neil Postman and Charles Weingartner, *Teaching as a Subversive Activity*, New York: Dell Publishing, 1969. See especially Chapter 5.

The link to an action gives much more traction to the teacher's task of shaping the training of effective professionals and citizens.

- One size does not fit all. One must shape the learning enterprise in a way that enables the student to start from where he or she *is*.

- Learning is a process, not an outcome. The process extends well outside the classroom and across time.

- To become relatively more learned is to make more meaning. Thus good students are good meaning-makers.

From the perspective of making meaning, the role of the teacher is to help students make meaning:

- The teacher can't make meaning *for* the students; only they can do it, and only for themselves. Students are not receivers or vessels for knowledge, waiting to be filled. They are processors for perceptions. The task for the teacher is to provide a stream of perceptions and opportunities to test their usefulness.

- Student-centeredness is not an option. Any hope for effective teaching must begin from an understanding of the uniqueness and diversity among learners in one's classroom.

- Ask often, tell seldom. Students make meaning to the extent that they discover ideas themselves. Rote memorization makes no meaning. One learns best that which one teaches oneself.

- Leading by exhortation and example may help students, but only to nudge students through the process of making meaning.

- Prepare for surprise. The meaning you had hoped to impart to students may not be the meaning they had acquired. Given the uniqueness of each person's filters, the meaning derived from the educational enterprise may vary considerably from one student to the next.

Where the teacher's views can help a student make meaning

Clarity about *how much* of one's views to insert into the learning experience is only part of the challenge. The other part is tactical, knowing *where and how* to insert them. The footprints of an effective teacher's views are found in the following classic areas:

1. **Course design.** The instructor gives direction through the selection of materials. Decisions about pacing add or diminish emphasis. Chapter 19, "Designing the Case Method Course," offers a range of considerations that can help the instructor establish a view. But the key idea is that all great course designs begin with the question, "What is your view?"

2. **Advance assignments to students.** Students pay fairly close attention to questions or guidance the instructor may offer in advance of class. Tread lightly here. Strong statements or highly directive assignment questions may signal your own view and pre-empt student exploration of alternatives.

3. **Class design.** One's overarching view guides the preparation for an individual class. Chapter 20, "Designing a case-method teaching plan," offers detailed suggestions. Any plan offers several opportunities for inserting one's views:

   a. **Teaching objectives.** The goals for each class frame the design for the day.

   b. **Question outline.** Rarely does a class follow a pre-set script. But the questions one frames in advance help the instructor envision an encounter with a range of views. My colleagues Jim Clawson and Sherwood Frey practice "pedagogical mapping" that conceives of a class less as a linear progression, and more like a series of contingent points where the discussion might turn—one can envision a branching tree. This richer view can help one foresee opportunities to insert views.

   c. **Closure.** The use of any summary or concluding comments lends the most visible opportunity to express a position. If anywhere, this is the place where the instructor most easily overdoes it. One might too easily pre-empt opportunities for students to make their own meaning. See Chapter 27, "Gaining closure," for more on this.

4. **Active discussion leadership.** In the hurly-burly of active class discussion, the teacher's view emerges in at least two areas:

   a. **Calling pattern.** Shortly after the course begins, an instructor learns that certain students are prone to make certain kinds of comments. The instructor can shape the views that emerge in a discussion by artfully recognizing students to speak in a useful pattern. It is not clear that Teacher A has a calling pattern

   b. **Questioning.** Ask often, tell seldom. The true believer (Teacher B) tended to tell, or assert his views. This shuts off discovery for the student.

But artful questioning in the classroom can shape views without sacrificing discovery for students.

5. **Setting ground rules.** Through writing and speaking, the teacher can shape views and student self-teaching by shaping the *process* of interaction in class discussion. In many case courses, one observes implicit or explicit ground rules such as these:

   a. **Punctuality.**

   b. **Preparation.**

   c. **No strong language.** Discussion leaders want debate with energy and some passion. But the words a student uses can quell or derail discussion. A student recently out of the Navy liberally sprinkled his class participation with shocking oaths that would have been standard vocabulary in the service, but are unacceptable in any professional setting. He was counseled to change his language and did so immediately.

   d. **No hostility.** Disparaging remarks based on gender, race, religion, sexual orientation, or nationality have a chilling effect on discussion and are unacceptable in professional circles.

Conclusion

Teachers A and B are polar extremes that invite us to imagine the profile of a teacher in the student centered middle. Neither too heavy in giving direction nor too light, this teacher intervenes with a view to promoting student self-discovery. My colleague, Jim Clawson, offers one metaphor for this teacher: the "electric energy grid manager," who sees supply and demand and aims to use the common resource (the grid or the classroom discussion) to optimize the learning for all. At any moment in the classroom there are numerous possible channels to get the energy focused on the need (the learning opportunity). The teacher's "view" is expressed in the choice of route, the timing of the routing decision, the pumping up or dampening of the total supply of energy, and the follow-up once the energy has arrived on target.

Politicians speak of the "power of the gavel," the power given to the leader of debates that has a strong influence on the course of the debates. Discussion leaders share a similar power. The solution is not to retreat into an "anything goes" style. Rather, the artistry of effective discussion leadership begins by making a careful assessment of the students' opportunities and capacities to make meaning and then exercising the range of teaching tactics to promote learning, consistent with your views.

Part 3
Developing Student
Centered Teaching Skills

Overview

Knowing what it means to be student centered is necessary but not sufficient to becoming a student centered discussion leader. In what dimensions might the instructor aim to grow? This part addresses in more detail some of the qualities necessary for effective student centered teaching.

- **Visualization** (Chapter 10). This chapter emphasizes the vital roles of thorough preparation and practice as foundations for developing a heightened sense of the possibilities in teaching materials and in the classroom.

- **"Mindfulness"** (Chapter 11). To be a student centered teacher requires vigilance against passive, mindless learning.

- **Dramatic consciousness** (Chapter 12). Part of the process of engaging students to participate actively is to draw on dramatic skills. To do this well requires more than just a mastery of techniques, but also a way of thinking about the actor and the audience.

- **A sense of humor** (Chapter 13). Humor is an extremely important device for engaging students, and more importantly, transforming their thinking about your subject.

- **Attention to useful styles of other teachers** (Chapter 14). Learning from exemplars is one of the most important avenues for personal growth as a teacher. This chapter suggests what to look for.

- **Seeking feedback from students** (Chapter 15). Listening to one's students affords important benchmarks for one's performance. What to listen for, and how, are surveyed in this chapter.

- **Mentorship** (Chapter 16). You never really learn something until you have to teach it to others. One way to strengthen your own mastery of teaching skills is to find the words, and the time, to help a colleague.

- **Using technology in a sensible way** (Chapter 17). New technology can help—or hinder—the student learning experience. Thus, using technology thoughtfully can contribute to your own growth as a discussion leader.

- **Telling others of your experience through a teaching portfolio** (Chapter 18). The process of describing your work helps build perspective, critical judgment, and clarity about your own path of development. This chapter describes using the teaching portfolio as a device for stimulating self-reflection.

Chapter 10
Seeing Discussion Possibilities[33]

Carl Sandburg, the poet, once interviewed the great baseball player, Babe Ruth, about his secret for hitting home runs. Ruth reportedly said, *"All I can tell 'em is I pick a good one and sock it. I get back to the dugout and they ask me what it was I hit and I tell 'em I don't know except it looked good."*[34]

Many good teachers offer self-assessments that boil down to Ruth's famous reply: banal or inscrutable, hardly the stuff from which others can take much direction. Why can't they say anything more meaningful about superior teaching? Plainly, one needs intelligence, empathy, energy, command, and many other fine qualities. But many instructors bear these qualities and yet struggle in the classroom. There is something extra, nearly indefinable, the "I only know it when I see it" quality.

Qualities of superior professionals

Malcolm Gladwell[35] explored the qualities that Wayne Gretzky, Yo-Yo Ma, and Charlie Wilson (a leading neurosurgeon) have in common. He argues that what distinguishes the superior performer from others is the capacity to see several possibilities in a particular setting and then to translate an assessment of those possibilities into action. Wayne Gretzky "sees not a setting but a number of situations." Yo-Yo Ma anticipates many possible variations in a cello performance so that even if a string breaks he can create an orderly execution of the piece. Charlie Wilson visualizes the presence of a tumor or aneurysm he can't quite see and successfully removes it. Gladwell calls these skills "the faculty of imagination." He writes that what sets superior performers apart is "their capacity to pick up on subtle patterns that others generally miss."

Gladwell's argument parallels lessons from other fields. Students of Aikido are taught the virtues of "soft eyes," seeing the whole rather than focusing on one segment. Chess players are taught to think strategically (many moves into the future) rather than myopically (one move at a time). GO players are taught to see the whole board, not

---

[33] My colleague Jim Clawson was particularly helpful in discussing with me the ideas in this chapter.

[34] Quoted in Carl Sandburg, "Notes for Preface," in *Harvest Poems*, New York: Harcourt Brace Jovanovich, 1960, page 11.

[35] See "The Physical Genius," *New Yorker,* August 2, 1999.

pieces of it. Managers are encouraged to consider the dynamics of their decisions (i.e., "systems thinking") rather than only immediate results.

Three qualities distinguish superior teachers:

- **Whole Vision.** This is a capacity to see holistically and to see beyond current circumstances toward possible future outcomes. I believe this is what Babe Ruth meant when he said, "It looked good." The *it* was what Ruth envisioned possibly doing with that ball. Superior case teachers "see" the case, the concepts, the students, and the setting all at once so they can orchestrate the connections. They envision rich possibilities not only in their cases, but also within the students whom they are teaching.

- **Real-time Judgment.** This is the capacity to interpret the implications of those possible future outcomes without stopping everything else. Babe Ruth did not measure the ball's velocity, the humidity of the air, or the myriad other factors that might affect the flight of the ball. Somehow he was able to judge the ball in the few hundredths of a second that it took to fly from the pitcher to home plate. Ruth was what baseball fanatics call a "natural," a born athletic genius. He allegedly did not practice, nor did he need to. But Gladwell suggests that for most superior performers (e.g. Yo-Yo Ma) relentless practice helps them to load experience into memory in a way that can be retrieved quickly for agile assessment. I see in superior teachers a habit of "practice through preparation" that enables them to interpret changing conditions quickly and with agility.

- **Decisive Action-taking.** Superior performers act quickly on the basis of their vision and assessment. Wayne Gretzky's famous saying is, "I skate to where the puck is going to be, not where it has been." Ruth did not just tap the ball, he *socked* it. Superior teachers intervene effectively in case discussions to lead to effective outcomes.

Working toward these qualities

A novice case teacher can adopt a number of practices to learn the ways of the superior performer, to build vision, agile assessment, and effective action-taking:

1. **Prepare thoroughly.** Know the teaching materials; know the students; know the environment[36]; know it all very well. Careful preparation helps one anticipate problems in the classroom, as well as unusual new opportunities. Solid preparation is the essential foundation for feeding the imagination (the fourth point below). The casual kind of preparation to teach absolutely undercuts all other efforts to build good teaching capabilities. One must prepare well beyond the suggestions offered in a case study teaching note. Most teaching notes are merely sketches of where a student's analysis might go. The teacher must replicate the student's likely analysis in order to discover analytical traps, ambiguities in the case, the various possible paths of student preparation, and unanticipated learning opportunities—most case writers leave it for the teacher to discover these rather than write the necessarily voluminous teaching note required to spell it all out.

2. **Create a teaching plan that you can "own."** Consider the virtue of internalizing or "owning" your teaching plan. It must be *your* plan, not someone else's. Case studies and other teaching materials are often accompanied by notes to the instructor that illustrate how the item might be taught in a discussion. Sometimes, the instructor can draw on the notes prepared by a colleague. Never rely mindlessly on the teaching notes of other instructors. [38] These notes are at best the guideposts toward a well-tailored teaching plan. At the same time, these teaching notes can help accelerate one's development of a workable teaching plan. All instructors should read such teaching notes to find out how someone else handles the materials. Knowledge is not your enemy; copycatting is. Start with notes prepared by others, and then develop your *own* plan.

3. **Stay flexible.** The dark side of preparing very thoroughly is that you over-learn the case and attempt to pack all your learnings into the class. This is content-centered teaching. Even though you may cover the content, your students may not

---

[36] To "know the environment" means more than knowing how the chalkboards work and where the thermostat is. It also requires familiarity with the mood of the students, culture of the school, the weather, the functioning of the local mass transit system, and major events taking place that might affect the quality of discussion. For more on this, see Chapter 29, "When Students are Silent."

[38] I have written many teaching notes, published to help other instructors prepare to teach. It may seem paradoxical therefore for me to advise that these should be avoided. My explanation lies in "rote": never rely mindlessly on the teaching notes of other instructors. These notes are at best the guideposts toward a well-tailored teaching plan.

learn. Admit the possibility that students may see things unknown to you. Retain enough flexibility in your plan to permit room for the unanticipated. As Yo-Yo Ma says to Gladwell, "Most successful performers improvise; they create something living." *Avoid becoming a captive of your own preparation.* Use your preparation to create "whole eyes," not closed eyes. The deep engagement one feels in preparing thoroughly is consistent with what Mihaly Csikszentmihalyi[39] describes as a feeling of "flow" or exhilaration among superior performers who are at their tasks. Thorough preparation contributes to one's "view" about the possibilities in a class discussion. At the same time, one must be careful to let the discussion evolve in a student centered way.

4. **Practice, teach a lot.** Practice creates judgment, consistency, and excellence. Also, there is a very steep experience curve in case teaching. The more you teach, the faster you ascend to higher levels of mastery. I'm not a big fan of sheltering the novice from the tempests of the case method classroom. Accumulated teaching time strongly predicts the capacity of the teacher to envision the possibilities in the next class. While experience is no guarantee of wisdom, it is a necessary ingredient.

5. **Feed your imagination.** Preparation helps but one could go much further into the background of the day's teaching materials by examining collateral readings in the mainstream of the field as well as quirky articles from the backwaters. Watch other teachers teach the same, or related, cases. Talk to other teachers about how they taught the same case. Practice envisioning sequences of questions and responses. Writing down some of these sequences might help you recall them. Finally, fight stress and fatigue--they dampen imagination and superior teaching. Try to go into class well rested and focused on the learning experience of the students.

Conclusion

Those who aspire to superior teaching must cultivate their capacities of whole vision, real-time judgment, and decisive action, in short, to "see a good one." Superior teachers are distinguished by their ability to see more in a teaching setting and by their ability to act decisively on what they see. From this perspective, Babe Ruth's famous reply was neither banal nor inscrutable. Seeing good discussion possibilities is not a matter of getting corrective lenses, but of *learning* a heightened level of perception and action-

---

[39] Mihaly Csikszentmihaly, *Flow: The Psychology of Optimal Experience*, New York: HarperCollins, 1990.

taking in the classroom—this is obtained by thorough preparation, by personal engagement with the subject, and by practice.

Chapter 11
"But Professor, I Did It By The Book":
Confronting *Mindless* Learning

"The best answers are never found in the back of the book."
                                             -- Jeff Millman[40]

"You can't have a high performance enterprise built on compliance. The essence of high performance is mindfulness—this is the foundation of agile response to uncertain events."
                                             --Alec Horniman[41]

A student writes an exam that follows the instructor's teaching points perfectly but misses a critical variation in the exam question causing the results to err markedly. Another student recites a formula from memory but cannot interpret it. A third student reliably offers numerical analysis in class but rarely questions assumptions or recommends decisions. A fourth student usually approaches you after class to verify "the right answer" to the case discussion. A fifth student uses student notes based on your discussion of the same case last year and considers copying a paper from the Internet for the final paper in your course. These behaviors challenge the teacher who cares about helping the student master subjects for professional life. A variety of forces drive these behaviors, but they probably have in common what social psychologist Ellen J. Langer calls *mindlessness*. If "professional mastery" means anything, it must include the ability to generate original work, to accommodate expected variations in problems, to reach outside of zones of familiarity, to focus on process rather than outcomes, and to accept the possibility of no single right answer. All of this requires *mindful learning*.

Perspectives on mindlessness and mindfulness

Ellen Langer's writing[42] on mindfulness springs from research that addresses behavior detached from its context. Types of mindlessness include these:

---

[40] Millman, the creative director of the Leo Burnett advertising agency, was quoted in an advertisement in *The Wall Street Journal*, 1991.
[41] Thanks go to my colleague Professor Alexander Horniman for stimulating conversation that led to this chapter.

- **"Automatic behavior."** Knowing CPR (cardio pulmonary resuscitation) so well that you can apply it automatically may be necessary to save a victim, but may not be sufficient. When one acts automatically, one may miss important signals such as a live electrical wire in the victim's hand, a damaged spine, or a mugger in the shadows, all of which can complicate the victim's rescue.

- **Category entrapment.** Categories help us understand why things happen as they do and may provide us a framework. They offer a stunted shorthand for clear and sometimes complex ways of thinking about the world. But categories can attain lives of their own, acquiring an elaborate superstructure or momentum perhaps entirely apart from the original state of the world from which the categories sprang. Mindlessness arises from a heavy dependence on categories or distinctions created in the past. As the great American baseball pitcher, Satchel Paige, once said, "It's not what you don't know that hurts you, it's what you know that just ain't so."

- **Acting from a single perspective.** Don't presume that there exists only one set of rules: a right way to cook a recipe (i.e., ignoring variations in tastes), a right way to play a game, a right way to market a product, a right way to finance a firm. Mindlessness does not admit variance or ambiguity.

Langer suggests that mindlessness arises from repetition, the loss of choice and control, an emphasis on snap judgments, a belief in limited resources, and a focus on goals rather than the process by which they are achieved. The costs of mindlessness are diverse and include a narrowing self-image, loss of control, learned helplessness, stunted potential, and unintended cruelty.

In contrast, Langer profiles *mindfulness* as including these attributes:

- The creation of new categories,

- Alertness to distinction,

- Sensitivity to different contexts,

- Openness to new ideas and novelty,

- Awareness of more than one perspective, and

- Orientation to the present.

---

[42] Ellen J. Langer, *Mindfulness,* Reading: Perseus Books, 1989. And Ellen J. Langer, *The Power of Mindful Learning,* Reading: Addison-Wesley, 1997.

An illustration of these qualities is offered by a survey of 40 MacArthur award winners by Denise Shekerjian. She sought to discover the attributes of this unusually gifted and prolific group of people. Among them was the avoidance of intellectual ruts, which become mindless patterns of thinking. Students have their own ruts, borne largely out of training and accumulated experience. These ruts tend to prevent students from listening well in class, and from achieving real mastery. To be creative, the student continually must step beyond what he or she already knows and thereby escape automatic behavior, entrapment by categories, and single perspectives. Shekerjian wrote, "Overfamiliarization with something—an idea, say, or a method, or an object—is a trap. Where creativity is concerned, that is the irony of skill: the more adept you are at something, the less likely you are to appreciate a varying interpretation; the greater your mastery of the skills and routines associated with a particular discipline, the less you will be tempted to generate new approaches."[43]

Implications for the discussion leader

What is an instructor to do with this? First, build your own familiarity with mindful teaching and learning. Langer's books are an excellent point of departure.[44]   Second, take action, both in the small and the large, to promote mindful learning. Here are some possibilities:

Ask often, tell seldom. A key principle of student centered teaching is that the role of the instructor is to promote student self-mastery of a subject through asking questions. Simply telling students "right answers" in an authoritative tone promotes mindlessness. Jerome Bruner wrote, "Telling children, and then testing them on what they have been told inevitably has the effect of producing benchbound learners whose motivation for learning is likely to be extrinsic to the task at hand--pleasing the teacher, getting into college, artificially maintaining self-esteem." Carl Rogers said, "The only learning which

---

[43] Denise Shekerjian, *Uncommon Genius: How Great Ideas are Born* (New York: Penguin Books, 1990), page 99.

[44] Consider the seven "myths" that Langer says undermine true learning, stifle creativity, silence questions, and diminish self-esteem:
  1. The basics must be learned so well that they become second nature.
  2. Paying attention means staying focused on one thing at a time.
  3. Delaying gratification is important.
  4. Rote memorization is necessary.
  5. Forgetting is a problem.
  6. Intelligence is "knowing what's out there."
  7. There are right and wrong answers.

significantly influences behavior is self-discovered, self-appropriated learning." The half-life of didactic learning is extremely short. Experiential learning lasts considerably longer. The discussion method teaches students to develop recommendations to realistic problems through direct engagement with those problems. Having to invent solutions to practical problems trains you to confront problems and also in the arts of problem solving and invention. Teaching-as-telling not only has a short impact, it produces the wrong behavioral responses from the student (e.g., ventriloquism, intellectual inflexibility, and plagiarism). Teaching-as-leading (i.e., leading through experiences) produces lasting learning because the student *makes meaning* and internalizes the ideas (for more on this, see Chapter 9).

Legitimize ambiguity and conditionality. In formal and informal ways the instructor can acknowledge that there may be several good alternatives to recommend to a problem, and that the ultimate choice will be conditional on the decision-maker's view of the current context, and the assessment of tradeoffs. Students frequently prefer certainty. And the instructor must not be so ambiguous and conditional as to undercut the students' faith that their studies will accomplish anything. For instance, one could solicit a variety of recommendations on a case study problem and then point out how the differing recommendations depend on differing outlooks. Langer writes, "For some, uncertainty represents an absence of personal control. From a mindful perspective, however, uncertainty creates the freedom to discover meaning. If there are meaningful choices, there is uncertainty…The theory of mindfulness asserts that uncertainty and the experience of personal control are inseparable."[45]

Don't over-assert. Related to the previous point must be an acknowledgement that every course is loaded with explanations about how the world works, of which some are more certain than others. But as the evolution of textbooks over time richly demonstrates, these explanations change. And scholars know that many of the assertions in these books are conditional, not absolute. It is intellectually more honest to represent to students that much remains uncertain, and that therefore they must arm themselves with skills of independent interpretation, analysis, and decision-making.

Stimulate critical thinking. Invite debate in study groups and in the classroom that triggers students' own assessments of tools and concepts, applications, assumptions, and recommendations. Critical thinking combats rote learning and promotes self-mastery.

---

[45] Langer (1997) *ibid.*, page 130.

Balance your emphasize process *and* outcome. There are no absolutely right answers in professional life. However, there are many wrong ones. Therefore professionalism resides in understanding all dimensions of a problem, getting the best data, using tools correctly and sensibly, questioning assumptions, looking for limitations or gaps in thinking, and thinking creatively about recommended solutions. Giving greater emphasis to process is not a formula for quick work and will frustrate students who want to skip along. But it strengthens the preparation of professionals and helps to limit wrong answers. Attention to process directly addresses Langer's insight that strong goal-orientation breeds mindlessness.

Create a stimulating learning context. Design courses and class assignments that break routine, provide a variety of decision settings, challenge students to invent fresh perspectives, and require students to take significant responsibility for their own learning. One could offer a blend of lectures, case studies, team-based papers, and applied simulations, such as negotiation exercises. The course should vary materially from year to year.

Some dissenting views

Any critique of the theory of mindfulness would summon up two classic objections. First, isn't mindfulness a luxury that necessarily builds upon rote learning, rules, and outcomes? Stated alternatively, don't you need to crawl before you can walk? For instance, one could cite the need to master the multiplication tables before high finance. If true, then mindful learning is really only the province of a small segment of education. In response one might point out that it is possible to learn most things mindfully—often learning only "sticks" when the student invents a pattern or framework that organizes what is to be learned. For instance, a child learns the multiplication tables by discovering the *pattern* of multiplicativity in the tables. Arguably this pattern is an important "Aha" that better prepares one for arithmetic calculation than does rote memorization. Knowing the multiplication tables is static mastery; *mindfully learning* the tables gives dynamic mastery and the foundation for action.

Second, it might be objected that overlearning and snap judgments are needed by society in a wide variety of situations such as professional athletics and emergencies. But the training in fields such as professional athletics and emergency service contradicts this. Actions may be quick, but the situation assessment is highly sophisticated and context-sensitive. Anyone who has coached a team will agree that the rote-overlearned athlete is rarely the leader on the field. The more debatable you find the points summarized here, the more I would encourage you to read Langer's books.

Conclusion

Why go to the trouble to confront mindlessness? Quite simply, mindlessness is costly.

- **Mindless learning** is inconsistent with the contribution to society that draws most educators into the classroom. The cost is increasingly apparent in a dynamic world where yesterday's answers may be less relevant today. Ultimately, one wants to feel proud of the people one prepares for professional life and of the enterprises and institutions those people will go on to create.

- **Teaching that promotes mindlessness** is a disservice to students, and short-changes their preparation.

Promote mindful learning in all you do.

Chapter 12
Teaching as Theatre: Finding One's Dramatic "Wits"

This fellow's wise enough to play the fool, and to do that well craves a kind of wit.
William Shakespeare
Twelfth Night Act 3, Scene 1

The Bard uses jesters toward serious ends. Jesters challenge decision makers to redefine problems, to consider new information, to abandon prejudices, and to recognize pervasive stupidity. Shakespeare shows that the wise person sometimes chooses to play the fool, to loosen up in carefully calculated ways, in order to convey deep ideas. His use of "wit" has a double meaning: humor *and* mindfulness. What is the role of dramatic wits in the classroom? How can an understanding of the actor's craft contribute to the success of teachers? What theatrical skills should a teacher seek to acquire?

Whether theatrics belong

Some academicians scorn the suggestion that teaching is *theatre*. It is argued that ideas should speak for themselves; their packaging or presentation should not matter. Learning is serious business. To infuse it with any notions of *entertainment* simply cheapens the scholarly enterprise. In addition, theatrical techniques in the classroom might create a dependency on the teacher, and weaken a student's reliance on self.

I take the view that using any techniques that aid and abet learning are well suited for the classroom. Learning requires a willing suspension of disbelief. Theatre helps an audience suspend disbelief. The best actors know that the play occurs not on stage, but in the minds of the audience. So it is with teaching: theatrical techniques in the classroom may help students apprehend an argument, see its flaws, consider its application to life, and tuck the lesson away for future use. Also, a little theatre can convey a sense of joy and passion for the subject that grabs attention and becomes infectious.

Perhaps the prime objection to teaching as theatre is personal, rather than institutional: "What if I make a fool of myself?" Virtually nothing in a professor's formal education prepares theatrical consciousness. Lame efforts to be more theatrical can end disastrously in gauche humor, wasted time and motion, and diminished respect. Against this possible outcome, why try? The best reason is to achieve greater personal satisfaction with one's work, as measured by learning among the students, and effective self-expression by the instructor. Always be genuine. Dramatic consciousness never fails when motivated by a sincere concern for student learning, and by one's own strengths and values. The market knows. Students can detect the difference between showmanship for its own sake and student-centered teaching. Moreover, they appreciate a little theatrical risk-taking. With some practice, you can learn a dramatic consciousness that is consistent with personal style and values and that promotes learning.

What wits to acquire

Teaching as theatre does not mean scripted speech, stage lights, or costumes. Instead, it is teaching with consciousness (or "wits") on at least the following dimensions:

- **Motion and stillness.** Hand gestures, raised eyebrows, walking around the room, even sitting can punctuate an idea that is in the air. Motion conveys energy and helps set the cadence of the class. Stillness creates tension or boredom.

- **Positioning in the room.** Moving around the room gives you a richer reading of the audience, and a better sense of who is seeking to contribute to the discussion. Professor C. Roland Christensen argued that *where* the instructor stood drew attention to student participants in the room. It has also been known to quicken the heartbeat of those students you stand near.

- **Speech and silence.** This is a consciousness about *what* to say, and *when*: the forcefulness of words and their timing. The choice of words helps to convey substance and to manage the process of the class. Also one must use the impressive power of silence. The comedian, Jack Benny, built his career on saying "Well…" and waiting the longest while before completing the thought.

- **Voice.** This is a choice about *how* to speak: loud, soft, modulated, flat. A physically diminutive instructor I know achieves great stature in the classroom through a self-confident and appropriately forceful voice.

- **Dress and props.** How the instructor dresses for class signals something about the instructor's stance in the educational enterprise. For instance, wearing a suit conveys a sense of formality, authority, and distance—qualities that a young instructor may want to express as part of an effort to gain leadership over young students. Wearing a suit may model the standard attire in certain professions and thereby help socialize students for life after school. In other settings, wearing a suit can backfire, such as when teaching an audience of professionals who are casually dressed, and aren't particularly impressed with suits anyway. Props (e.g., reading glasses, retractable chalk holders, and pointers) can assist with dramatic expression, though they must be used judiciously lest they dissolve into weary gimmicks.

- **Entry and exit.** This is a consciousness about making effective *transitions*. The best transitions are motivated by clarity about what you are leaving, where you are heading, and why. "Every exit is an entrance somewhere else," said Tom Stoppard in his play, *Rosencrantz and Guildenstern are Dead.* Actors and teachers use these transitions to help define their role

- **Humor and gravity.** An unremitting diet of light or heavy gets tedious. The teacher must develop a consciousness around variation from one to the other. As Shakespeare's jesters illustrate, humor and gravity can coexist; each can amplify the other. One of the prominent practitioners of this was physicist and Nobel Laureate, Richard P. Feynman, who peppered his dense lectures with jokes and anecdotes.

These elements suggest that dramatic wits, the intuition about what to do and when, are complex and potentially powerful. Some may be born with an intuitive grasp of these dimensions. But most instructors will need to learn them. Why should one make such an investment?

Where dramatic mastery can help

Dramatic consciousness can serve the instructor in a variety of ways. Here are some examples:

- **Managing classroom tension.** The effective teacher uses tension to promote learning. Tension can motivate students to solve a problem and sharpen a grasp of the issues. I have seen all of the dramatic wits used to manage tension.

- **Building a healthy learning culture.** Dramatic wits can help set high expectations for performance, sustain a high energy level in the room, challenge lazy thinking, spur creativity, and encourage debate.

- **Restoring a sense of novelty.** The routine of teaching can create a feeling of being on autopilot, a dryness, a sense of "been there, done that," an impatience with the process of student mistakes, a kind of tuning-out or loss of awareness of the students. Often this stems from a repetitive reliance on old notes, familiar teaching materials, and comfortable concepts. Dramatic wits permit interesting variations in performance that may not be immediately apparent to the audience but that can render the teaching assignment vastly more interesting and enjoyable.

- **Promoting gracefulness.** Awkwardness is hard on both instructor and students. One may see wasted motion or no motion at all; hear a voice that quavers; observe posture suggesting fear or discomfort; and notice a problem of what to do with the hands. The instructor's awkwardness can distract the audience from his or her ideas. And it can hamstring the achievement of *command* or ownership of the classroom. Dramatic wits can build comfort and self-confidence in the teaching task.

A resource for developing one's dramatic wits

An excellent book by Uta Hagen, *A Challenge for the Actor*,[46] lends numerous insights into how an instructor might build an appreciation for the theatrical aspects of teaching. She surveys acting techniques, offers 10 exercises, and discusses preparation of a role. Hagen argues that all good acting begins from a mastery of a role derived from homework, rehearsal, and intense concentration. Ultimately this mastery *expresses a view* by the artist about the world. Here is a sampler of her possible lessons for teachers:

1. **Integrate ideas and action.** Hagen writes,

   > "It is often during moments when our objectives and behavior seem routine, when the conflict is not self-evident, that our concentration can flag and the attention will stray—into the audience or to irrelevant areas of our personal lives. As a young actor I used to kick myself, blaming such moments on poor concentration. It was simply that I hadn't learned what to concentrate on."[47]

   Hagen argues that an actor should concentrate first on the *ideas* underlying the role and the play. One should not separate thought and action.

2. **Suspend expectations.** Hagen described overcoming a dry spell in her career by building a sense of fresh expectation. She found that great actors have

---

[46] Uta Hagen, *A Challenge for the Actor*, New York: Scribner, 1991.
[47] *Ibid.* page 108.

"utter spontaneity and unpredictability of their actions. You believed their existence in the present, that everything was happening to them from moment to moment, as if for the first time. They seemed as surprised by the events that stormed in on them during the course of the play as the audience. This was what I wanted to find in my own work."[48]

Her solution was to suspend her own expectations about her role and instead strive to re-create the character's expectations.

"The actor faces one of his most difficult problems: how to repeat the selected actions at every performance from moment to moment, as if for the first time. …It is achieved by a suspension of knowledge of what is to come, by 'forgetting' everything except what is needed at the moment with the profound innocence that is part of an actor's soul."[49]

Having discovered this, she writes,

"My passion for acting returned, never to desert me again, once I had understood how to suspend knowledge of what was to come by unearthing the character's expectations. I was finally able to use my imagination to achieve the innocence and faith needed to find a new life in rehearsals and to be spontaneously alive on stage when executing the actions from one moment to the next, caught up by the surprises that move in on me. Then every performance becomes a challenge, a new adventure of playing as if for the first time instead of a repetition of the night before. I can honestly claim that I will be more alive on stage at the end of a year's run than I was at the beginning. The effort does not exhaust me—it exhilarates me! If you want to soar, try it: surprise yourself."[50]

If learning requires a willing suspension of disbelief by the student, then Hagen would offer complementary advice to instructors: "suspend expectations," the

---

[48] *Ibid.* page 123.
[49] *Ibid.* page 164.
[50] *Ibid.* page 128.

presuppositions about who the students usually are, what they usually need, how they usually will encounter the subject, what is usually good for them, etc.—this is the mentality of the teacher-centered teacher. To suspend expectations is to be student-centered; it is to focus on the unique challenges of student learning in the present circumstances, rather than on teaching.

3. **Prepare thoroughly.** At numerous points in the book, Hagen attacks the notion that good acting just happens. Rather, it springs from deep study, reflection, and rehearsal. This is consistent with what we observe in university teaching: it does not just happen, but rather results from relentless preparation. Hagen's advice on preparation is instructive. At the outset she urges the actor to "READ THE PLAY—in its entirety."[51] "In preparation for a role, we must explore and give special attention to the play's theme, conflict, the alignment of its adversaries and our character's relation to them, its main action, and its motivating causes."[52]

Homework begins when the actor picks up the script for the first time, and does not stop until the end of the final performance. Homework includes extensive background reading on the play, the playwright, the history of the play's setting, intellectual questions or conflicts raised in the play, etc. She advocates keeping a journal or notebook of reflections, questions, reminders, etc. The actor must "score the role" by exploring such fundamental questions as "Who am I?" "What are my circumstances?" "What are my relationships?" "What do I want?" "What's in my way?" "What do I do to get what I want?"[53]

4. **Before your entrance, clear the "runway."** Hagen argues that one must create the space to shift into a role before making an entrance:

> "A correct preparation entails clearing the runway by creating
> an area of privacy and stillness in the wings or on stage, having
> arrived there in plenty of time, blocking out existing

---

[51] *Ibid.* page 233.

[52] *Ibid.* page 242.

[53] I concur that thorough preparation is vital. But one can overlearn the material to the point of losing sight of the teaching aims. Donald Hambrick wrote, "Some risks are associated with being exceedingly experienced on a topic you are teaching. The chief risk is that you will lose all sight of what a newcomer to the material most needs to know and how it is best imparted...A basic challenge in teaching is to draw a distinction between what you know about a subject and what is important for your students to know. The more you know, the more complicated this challenge." (Donald C. Hambrick, "Teaching as Leading," in *Researchers Hooked on Teaching*, Rae Andre and Peter J. Frost, eds., Thousand Oaks CA: Sage Publications, 1997, page 253.

distractions and unrelated realities by concentrating on the three things essential to a smooth takeoff. We 'rev up' by giving attention to: where did I just come from and what was I doing there? Where am I right now and what am I doing here? Where am I going and what do I want to do there? If I follow through, I will be in flight for my journey in the play."[54]

It helps to take time before each class to consider where the students and the course are coming from, where the class will be today, and where students and the class will head from here.

These and other reflections address the fundamental challenge of mastering a role. Hagen, in effect, invites teachers to consider how they seek to define their own role in relation to their students, and to structure dramatic behavior accordingly.

Conclusions

Good teaching reflects dramatic consciousness that is implemented thoughtfully, tastefully, and in reasonable doses. Teaching and acting have much in common. The instructor who strives to develop an effective teaching style would do well to attend to the many dimensions of the "wits" to which Shakespeare referred. One can stimulate development of them through a program that includes elements such as these:

- **Reading.** Hagen's book is a good point of departure into a large literature on training of actors. One's colleagues in the field of drama can suggest other readings.

- **Observation.** Exemplars help illuminate what is possible. But one must watch with discipline and careful attention.[55] Remember that effective acting and teaching appear to be effortless. Therefore, some of the best insights from observation will be the most elusive.

- **Coaching.** I have known of teaching colleagues who have benefited from working with acting and voice coaches, which university drama departments can help find. Alternatively, one can try peer-based coaching available in faculty teams committed to observation or in community organizations such as Toastmasters, which promotes effective public speaking skills.

---

[54] Hagen *Ibid.* page 149.
[55] For tips, see Chapter 14, "How to Observe a Colleague Teach a Case."

Dramatic wits are dearly acquired, usually over the entire span of a career. Persistence is needed, as is the courage to "play the fool" now and then. But judging from the excellent teachers I have observed, the payoff is handsome.

Chapter 13
Transforming Thought:
The Role of Humor in Teaching

Mrs. Teasdale:	"I was with my husband to the very end."
Groucho Marx:	"Huh! No wonder he passed away."
Mrs. Teasdale:	"I held him in my arms and kissed him."
Groucho Marx:	"Oh, I see. Then it was murder."

-- *Duck Soup*, 1933.[56]

"This I conceive to be the chemical function of humor: to change the character of our thought."

-- Lin Yutang[57]

In his classic film, *Duck Soup*, Groucho Marx transforms a widow's conventional words of sorrow into a take-off on the American phrase, "If looks could kill..." He shows how humor can change the way one thinks about problems and situations. Lin Yutang calls the transformational effect of humor, "chemical," suggesting the effect of a catalyst, perhaps silent but inexorable and often dramatic. Teaching is all about transforming a student's thinking. Therefore, humor belongs in the teaching toolkit, and deserves to be used frequently.

The problem is that the substance of what most instructors have to teach isn't very funny. Effective use of humor, therefore, must rely on *delivery*. Nothing in one's professional training prepares for this. Yet great teachers display the ability to use humor effectively in the pursuit of learning. Where does one acquire such skills? How should humor be used? What traps are to be avoided? This chapter reflects on these and related questions.

---

[56] Kanfer (2000) pages 38-39. The release by Paramount Pictures of *Duck Soup* dramatically raised the bar for comedy in film. As a mark of its impact, that film remains today among the American Film Institute's 100 Greatest Pictures. Seen from 2002, the film retains a fundamental sparkle, a ceaseless stream of verbal surprise that relentlessly shifts the viewer's point of view about characters and plot. One has the sense of professional actors having a whale of a good time. At the core of this team was Groucho Marx, an extraordinary wit, of whom Woody Allen later wrote, "He is simply unique in the same way Picasso and Stravinsky are, and I believe, his outrageous, unsentimental disregard for order will be equally funny a thousand years from now. In addition to all this, he makes me laugh."

[57] Lin Yutang (1895-1976) was a Chinese-American writer, translator, and editor.

How humor can improve the learning experience

Research suggests that humor promotes learning. Ronald Dieter (1998) reviewed the literature and concluded, "The use of humor should be a teaching tool that, if effective, will increase the amount of *what* is taught that is actually learned by students." He cited benefits such as these:

- **Attention.** Humor stimulates students to sit up and listen.

- **Connection.** Humor can help students see patterns, connect examples with concepts, or find inconsistencies. As Lin Yutang suggests, humor is a catalyst that can help stimulate making intellectual connections.

- **Retention.** A tag or connection of some sort significantly helps ideas stick— humor serves this purpose. A professor helps undergraduates remember a key figure of German 19th century history by ludicrously comparing Otto von Bismarck to a jelly-filled doughnut.[58]

- **Creativity and critical thinking.** William Fry, professor emeritus of psychiatry at Stanford, says, "Creativity and humor are identical. They both involve bringing together two items which do not have an obvious connection, and creating a relationship."[59]

- **Social cohesion.** Every case method classroom is a learning community. Humor helps build the sense of community and creates rapport between teacher and students. Erich Segal wrote, "Laughter is a vital sign of humanity …a social gesture which binds the community and integrates society."[60] By drawing the listener into the circle of a joke, the instructor seems to say, "You are important."

- **Assessment.** Humor can serve as a type of teaching sonar: the time it takes for a laugh to follow a witticism is a telltale about the students. The ability to laugh hints at levels of intelligence, tension, and energy in the room, the presence of distractions, and generally the level of engagement that students bring to the learning task.

- **Awareness of self and others.** Building self-knowledge is one of the fundamental aims of education. Raj Persaud writes, "You have to be aware of your own sense of tension and puzzlement as the joke is told. In other words,

---

[58] In some regions of the U.S., "Bismarck" is the common name for a type of jelly-filled doughnut.
[59] Quoted from an essay, "Cultural Values and Their Impact on Business Practices," found on the Internet at www.tuckerintl.com/General/Readings/Humor/HumorP3.html.
[60] Segal (2000) pages 23-24.

personal memory, self-awareness, and therefore consciousness appear to be functions at the heart of joke understanding." He writes that to understand cartoons requires a "theory of mind," or sense of what is going on in other people's minds.[61]

- **Fun.** Humor raises the enjoyment of a challenging activity and makes it easier to complete assigned tasks.

- **Health.** Medical research finds that laughter reduces stress, exercises the heart, and increases activity in the immune system.[62] Norman Cousins (1990 and 1991) described the power of laughter to reduce pain in his personal battle with spinal disease.

Finding a personal style (and material) for teaching with humor

The major concern for most teachers is uncertainty about their own style of delivery, and how to improve it. Finding a style is not an engineering problem. It cannot be forced. One grows into it. One needs to develop a mental orientation toward humor, and then exercise it regularly, like an athlete would train for a contest. Humor needs to be a part of the professional's day. Consider the following ways to bring it into your day:

- **Be receptive.** Humor favors the prepared mind. Freud argued that humor springs from an emotional impulse. One needs to be emotionally ready to let humor rise.

- **Read.** Consume written humor in many small doses, rather like the advantage of a time-release capsule. Humor anthologies and short magazine articles are ideal for this.

- **Watch and listen.** Film and television let one watch the pros at work.[64] The American Film Institute's list of 100 Great Comedies is a useful point of

---

[61] Persaud (2000).

[62] William Fry (see Fry and Salaheh 1986) argues that laughter is a good source of cardiac exercise. Herbert Lefcourt (1986, 2000) of University of Waterloo found increased levels of defenses against viral and bacterial infections in people following a period of laughter induced by humorous recordings. Lee Berk (1998) of University of California found increases in immunoglobulins and interferon, increased activity of natural killer cells, and reductions in levels of cortisol (an immune system suppressor.)

[64] The nightly opening comedy monologue on late night television talk shows is a source of topical humor, repeatable before a broad audience. Some of these monologues are available on audio tape and CD-ROM, see, for example, the CD by Jerry Seinfeld (1998).

departure.[65] The AFI list embraces a very wide range of what qualifies as humor. Find what you like, so that you can target your learning.[66]

- **Search.** Branch out from the classics in digital and print media. The Internet is loaded with sources of humor.[67] Unfortunately a great deal of the humor on the Internet is inappropriate for the classroom and/or simply not that good. Magazines such as *The New Yorker* and *Reader's Digest* print promising humor regularly. An important source of good new humorous material is word-of-mouth communication. Find colleagues who enjoy humor and use it well in conversation and in class. Watch them at work, if you can.

- **Invent rather than imitate.** The point of searching for good humor is not to absorb a repertoire of canned jokes, but rather to stimulate your own capacity for invention. The ability to invent humor spontaneously in the classroom is vastly preferable to parroting the work of others.

- **Try. Above all, think critically.** Reflect on what works for you, your values, style, and situation. Practice humor with our family and friends who will likely groan (because that's what family does) but will also give you a safe environment to try. Explain why you are doing it, and ask for their feedback and encouragement. The practice of humor is not a one-size-fits-all phenomenon. Tailoring is crucial. The point of critical reflection is to sharpen your capacity to make rapid decisions about whether to exploit a possibly humorous opportunity, and how.

Some stylistic considerations: jokes versus wit

The instructor might reflect on the pros and cons of the two basic kinds of classroom humor. Jokes are set-piece episodes of humor. A favorite teacher of mine used jokes very effectively as an opening monologue to the class. Though a sober personality, he delivered the monologue effectively. This had the effect of warming up the room each day, and gave students an incentive to get to class on time. There is a disadvantage of using jokes though. They can halt discussion. Jokes are usually teacher-centered: the teacher is the performer. Don't let joke-telling dampen and derail class discussion.

---

[65] See www.afi.com.

[66] If you don't know where to begin, I recommend starting with comedy films of the 1930s and 1940s, the golden era of "screwball comedy." For an excellent discussion of screwball comedy, see the comments by an unknown author at Hampshire College at
http://hamp.hampshire.edu/~pswF94/cusp/nostalgia/screw.html.

[67] See, for instance, www.comedycentral.com.

Wit is spontaneous, and fits more easily into the flow of discussion. It springs from students' words or ideas and engages students in a new perspective. Though it requires careful listening to recognize an opportunity for wit, good listening is a universal requisite for good teaching and should be cultivated as a skill. The possible downside of wit is that it can motivate some instructors to speak impulsively. Saying the first thing to come into one's mind invites embarrassment. The witty instructor needs to cultivate self-discipline about making humor.

Implementing one's style of humor

Having a style of humor is a necessary but insufficient condition for promoting learning. How you implement the style is crucial.

- **Be prepared.** Delivering humor well depends on being alert and receptive to the audience. Try to enter the classroom rested and composed. To be at your best, take a "breather" before class to focus your attention on the upcoming discussion and its possible opportunities.

- **Be brief.** Shakespeare wrote, "Brevity is the soul of wit."[68]

- **Look for a new way of thinking, and shape a surprise around it.** Humor is a means of helping students find a new and *surprising* perspective on a familiar subject.

- **Tailor your wit to the audience, setting, and especially language and culture.** Shakespeare wrote, *"A jest's prosperity lies in the ear/ Of him that hears it, never in the tongue/ Of him that makes it."* [69] Success depends on the parties to the joke. The challenge, therefore, is to craft humor that is appropriate to the listener and the situation. Crafting a style of humor for class depends on knowing the student. The leading reason why humor falls flat in the classroom is a mismatch between the jest and the audience.

  o **Spanning national borders.** Differences in language and culture demand careful tailoring. Comic devices such as irony, deadpan, slang, and allusion may escape students entirely. Foreign students may be several seconds (or minutes) behind the speaker in processing the words and their

---

[68] William Shakespeare, *Hamlet* (Act II, Scene 2). Ironically, these famous words were spoken by Polonius, a character hardly known for his brevity.

[69] William Shakespeare *Love's Labor's Lost* (Act V, Scene 2).

meaning which is sure to challenge the timing of surprise   In these circumstances, it will help if you try to speak slower, use more widely understood vocabulary, and perhaps rely on cartoons or slides that contain written jokes that can be projected onto a screen and left there long enough for the audience to grasp them. Be aware that all of the sources suggested here yield U.S.-centric humor. Match the right kind of humor to your audience and the learning opportunity.

- o **Older vs. younger.** As the population in developed countries continues to age, university instructors may see a graying of their students. The hip humor of twenty-somethings may elude middle-aged or senior-aged students.

- o **Degree candidates versus practitioners.** Increasingly practitioners return to universities for professional training. Their frame of reference as to what is important—and funny—will differ from the uninitiated.

- **Shelter the weak.** In stark contrast to the practice of most nightclub comedians, the student-centered teacher should be very careful in bantering or jesting with weak students. One's object should be to promote student learning, not entertain the strong.

- **Use self-deprecating humor gingerly.** Some comedians, such as Woody Allen, rely on humor taken at their own expense. This draws the listener in for a surprise. Self-deprecating humor is disarming. It can work in the classroom if the teacher enjoys students' respect, has some authority in a body of knowledge or in the school hierarchy, or has a long legacy at the school. Its disarming quality is especially effective in dealing with student fears about the course, instructor, or subject. It seems to say, "I'm human, fallible, and approachable" and therefore invites engagement between the student and teacher. But it can undercut the teacher among those who are wary. One should be reluctant to use self-deprecating humor until the teacher's leadership is established and circumstances call for it.

- **Avoid hostile humor, bathroom humor, or obscenity.** Humor that makes fun of religious or ethnic groups, gender-based differences, height, age, or region speaks more about the anger and/or preoccupations inside the speaker than about the learning focus of the class. Whether or not these sentiments seem widely shared, do you really need to reveal them to students? Put-downs and attacking humor could easily isolate the teacher—the very opposite of what a discussion leader should be trying to achieve. Most U.S. universities and professional organizations would find this kind of humor unacceptable. If insulting your students isn't bad enough, hostile humor can trigger sanctions under U.S. laws and regulations prohibiting discriminatory behavior.

- **Use supporting media where helpful.** If you are not comfortable telling jokes or bantering with students, consider using other devices to inject some humor into your class. Cartoons are widely used by many effective instructors.[70] Video segments can afford another important source of support. One could draw on short excerpts from films, television skits, monologues etc. Teachers have used skits from *Saturday Night Live* and *Monty Python* as "breathers" between classes.[71] See also the incomparable *Who's on First?* by Abbott and Costello.

- **Don't laugh at your own jokes.** The comedian's deadpan visage is a staple of most comedy acts. Freud remarked on this and noted that it is through the laughter of the other person that the speaker enjoys the humor in his or her own words. To laugh at your own jokes suggests that you are focused inward (i.e., not student-focused) and that you are pursuing humor egotistically. Students readily laugh *at rather than with* the egotist. Usually a comedian smiles; occasionally he chuckles or snorts; but he never *laughs*.

- **Respect copyrights and acknowledge the creativity of others.** Representing humor that you have appropriated from others as your own feeds a culture of plagiarism. Liberally acknowledge the creative work of others. Also, it is vital to respect copyright restrictions in your country. In the United States, an established convention is that the display of copyrighted work by a professor in face-to-face teaching activities is either not an infringement or would likely be "fair use" of copyrighted material—this would permit the general practices outlined here, including display of cartoons and video segments that you either recorded at home or rented from a commercial supplier. It is also true that the dividing line between fair use and infringement is blurry and changes as the courts hand down new decisions over time. When in doubt, consult an attorney—many universities will not compensate professors for damages or awards of infringement claims against them.[72]

---

[70] One of the best sources of cartoons is the website associated with *The New Yorker* magazine, www.cartoonbank.com. Other reasonable sources of cartoons are United Media (http://www.unitedmedia.com/editoons/), *Washington Post* (http://www.washingtonpost.com/wp-dyn/politics/columns/), and *New York Times* (www.nytimes.com/diversions/cartoons).

[71] The commercially available videotape series *The Best of Saturday Night Live* is a fertile source of short humorous video clips. Business school instructors may find one part of the series, *SNL Goes Commercial* (Starmaker, #630002), to offer material relevant to a managerial audience.

[72] I thank my colleague G. David Ibbeken, copyright attorney, for his insights regarding "fair use" of copyrighted material and the appropriateness of display of humor material.

Conclusion

Great humorists like Groucho Marx function as teachers in the sense that they bring a new perspective to familiar subjects. Lin Yutang calls this a "chemical" transformation in thinking, like a catalyst: surprising, and often powerful. Humor helps learning. Yet most instructors go to work without it. One hears the usual objections such as "It's just not me." "I can't tell jokes." "It doesn't work in my course." Underlying most objections is a basic fear of failure, of looking absurd before one's students. But usually it is in the *trying* that one demonstrates the clear effort to engage students and promote learning, qualities that most students will endorse.

Suggested Readings and References

Berk, R.A., *Professors are from Mars, Students are from Snickers*, Madison WI: Mendota Press, 1998.

Cousins, Norman, *Head First: The Biology of Hope and the Healing Power of the Human Spirit*, New York: Penguin Books, 1990.

Cousins, Norman, *Anatomy of an Illness as Perceived by the Patient*, New York: Bantam Doubleday, 1991.

Dieter, Ron, "Why Use Humor in the Classroom?" *Teaching at ISU*, Nov/Dec 1998, Vol. 11, No. 2, found at www.cte.iastate.edu/newsletter/november 98/humor.html.

Freud, Sigmund, "Wit and its Relation to the Unconscious," in *The Basic Writings of Sigmund Freud*, A.A. Brill (trans.), New York: Modern Library, 1995.

Fry, William F., and Waleed A. Salameh (eds.) *Handbook of Humor and Psychotherapy: Advances in the Clinical Use of Humor*, Professional Resource Exchange; ISBN: 0943158192, November 1986.

Kanfer, Stefan, ed., *The Essential Groucho: Writings by, for and about Groucho Marx*, New York: Vintage Books, 2000.

Lefcourt, Herbert F., *Humor and Life Stress: Antidote to Adversity*, Springer Verlag; ISBN: 0387962492, April 1986.

Lefcourt, Herbert F., *Humor - The Psychology of Living Buoyantly (The Plenum Series in Social/Clinical Psychology)*, Plenum Pub Corp; ISBN: 0306464071, October 2000.

Persaud, Raj, "Why you laugh your head off," *Electronic Telegraph* 16 November 2000, www.personal.eunet.fi/pp/liikan/Insets/ExtractPages/Why-laugh-you-head-off.html.

Pyper, Andrew, "Laugh Factor," *Enroute*, October 2001.

Remnick, David, and Henry Finder, eds., *Fierce Pajamas: An Anthology of Writing from the New Yorker*, New York: Random House, 2001.

Segal, Erich, *The Death of Comedy*, Boston: Harvard University Press, 2000.

Seinfeld, Jerry *I'm Telling You for the Last Time* Uni/Universal Records; ASIN: B00000AFGO, 1998.

Chapter 14
How to Observe a Colleague Teach a Case

"You can observe a lot just by watching."
-- Yogi Berra

Observation is one of the most important means by which one learns to teach. It is hard, fully engaged work. This chapter offers some tips for making this a more fruitful use of time.

Begin with a learning attitude.[73] We all carry in our minds models of Great Teachers or our own past teaching successes. These can filter out good examples to be found in the teaching by other colleagues. My advice is to suspend preconceptions at the outset.

Next, it is important to get up to speed on the class one is about to observe. This entails at least two steps: reading the case and teaching note, and getting the instructor's advance thinking about the class.[74] What are the possibilities in the material, the aims of the course, and the immediate needs of the students? What are the strengths and weaknesses of the case? Where are students on the path of intellectual development in the course? What are the instructor's goals and plan for the class session? What tools or concepts have the students most recently confronted? How will this case prepare the students for the next step in their journey?

What to look for

It pays to get to the classroom early and gain a sense of the immediate context of the class. Give particular attention to the energy level, attitude, and apparent preparedness of the students. Other little details such as temperature, lighting, seating arrangement, and cleanliness of the room affect teaching. How does the instructor handle these teaching challenges posed by the classroom itself? When the class starts, observe at least five processes:

---

[73] Observing a colleague as part of a promotion process entails a different attitude; the comments in this chapter suppose that self-improvement alone is the aim.

[74] It is equally interesting to take the *student's* view, and read only the assigned teaching material for the day, i.e., without peeking into the mind of the teacher. In this chapter I advocate the teacher's view simply for the sake of understanding the design logic of the person you are observing.

1. **The questioning process.** Keep a list of the questions and statements made by the instructor. What was the flow of the questions? Were they pointed and directive (searching for specific answers) or more open-ended (inviting the student to reveal a larger pattern of thinking)? How did the instructor blend telling and inquiring? Did the instructor settle for technical answers or push the student to offer insights useful for the decision-maker? Finally, where did the questioning appear to respond to the students? Where else did it follow an apparent pre-determined pattern?

2. **The process of recognizing students.** Before the class begins, one can draw a map of seating in the room. As the class proceeds, check off the students who are called upon. By the end of class, you will have the footprints of the instructor's calling pattern. This may reveal a strategy of breadth or focus in the way the instructor drew on the students. After class, you can invite the instructor to comment on the calling choices he or she made.

3. **The process of graphic presentation.** Notes on graphic process could include a rough sketch of the chalkboards at the end of class, the key lessons from PowerPoint and   videotape presentations (and their time length), and the structure and insights of spreadsheet models. How did the use of these enhance the class discussion? Did they create discussion energy or focus? How were the chalkboard or PowerPoint slides organized?

4. **The process of the instructor's movement around the classroom.** Instructors mobilize students with proximity and action. Does he or she stay rooted in front of the chalkboard, or roam the aisles? Is the movement predictable or surprising? How does the instructor motion with hands and facial expressions? Is the movement slow or fast? Where did the tempo of movement change? How do students seem to react to this movement? To record the movement of the instructor, I sketch the paths on the map of the classroom that I prepared for the calling patterns.

5. **The performance process.** If teaching is a performing art, one can make marginal notes on elements such as the instructor's entry and exit, use of humor and tension, and sense of closure. The focus of these comments is not with entertainment, but rather with the way in which the instructor gains and uses audience attention. See Chapter 12 for comments on dramatic techniques.

There may be other processes worth following as well. But these five will almost certainly yield useful insights. The price of these insights is only a tired writing hand by the end of the class period. Plainly, serious observation of a teacher is a lot of work. Some colleagues claim to be able to glean these insights without writing a word. I'm not blessed with such detailed recall so I have opted for sore hands, and many notes.

The final phase of any classroom observation should be a debriefing with the instructor. My first question is how he or she thought the class went. What may have seemed to be a muted discussion may have been an enormous breakthrough from the instructor's perspective. To walk in the instructor's shoes will put much of what you observed in a new light. Next, I offer my two or three most interesting observations, and invite the instructor to comment or explain. Finally, at most schools the classroom remains a relatively private preserve of the instructor; if you hope to visit again, a collegial expression of thanks is in order.

Observing other teachers is indispensable for novice discussion leaders and is a useful way for seasoned instructors to retain their edge.[75] Following the steps outlined here, the total time commitment per class observed is probably between three and four hours. For most busy instructors this carries a high opportunity cost. The key is to plan to observe as far as a year ahead and make commitments.

Adopt the "best practices"

The final step in learning-by-observation must be to implement the good in what you saw. The emphasis must be on "the good": never dispense with a critical point of view in your observations. Some teaching techniques will not be consistent with your teaching style or values. Others won't be appropriate for the particular context you face. Still others will be consistent and appropriate, but may represent a very big stretch for you—consider implementing these by degrees. But without your own attempt to implement what you observed, there can be no growth. Howard Aldrich said,

> The problem with the role model is that some of the techniques that are good to use in teaching are very hard to learn by just observing somebody, because they are subtle. People tend to assume that teaching is intuitive and obvious and that it

---

[75] To be a solo case teacher or discussion leader at a school dominated by the lecture method would seem to condemn one to a career of growth without observation. Professional networking and informal alliances with discussion leaders at other schools can help fill this void, as can attendance at teaching workshops offered at professional conferences and the major case method schools.

is a normal, every day behavior. I tell my students that you can spend a lot of time reading about teaching practices, but reading is no substitute for practice…You can't do it simply by watching. Unreflective observing just doesn't work.[76]

In short, *practice* of observed "best practices" is vital. To stimulate good implementation, make notes that highlight these practices, and that will remind yourself to consider adopting them the next time you teach. These notes might cover:

- **The five classroom processes** that were outlined above. What about the instructor's management of these processes might you experiment with?

- **Classroom context.** This might include the arrangement of seating, the heating and lighting, and the use of name cards. Consider how the instructor shaped the classroom context to his or her requirements. Do you do this?

- **Plan for teaching** the same or similar material, how one asks questions, and in what order. What aspects of the teaching plan might you try?

- **Course design.** Each class meeting represents another stage in the unfolding of a course plan. What did today's class tell you about the overarching design of the course? What about this design might benefit the design of your own course?

- **Course or school culture.** Each day an instructor has opportunities to reinforce valuable norms that promote learning. In the class you observed, what norms did the instructor reinforce, and how? What is the role of learning norms in your course? How might you reinforce them?

With a little clarity about what you might try, go ahead and try it.

---

[76] Quoted in Diane Baird, "A teaching champion: An interview with Howard Aldrich," UltiBase articles, http://ultibase.rmit.edu.au/develop/Articles/june97/aldri1.htm.

Chapter 15
Taking Stock: Evaluations From Students

A packet of student evaluations of you and your course arrive on your desk at the end of the season. This packet is one of the tell-tales of larger forces of change in higher education. Virtually all schools are giving more attention to the quality of teaching and course designs. Evaluations have gotten longer and more detailed. They carry more weight in decisions about promotion, tenure, and compensation. Qualitative comments from students seem to carry more bite. The pressures to please recruiters and other clients, the advent of national rankings of schools by major magazines, and generally the trend toward consumerism in education are some of the tectonic forces at work here.

Many instructors view student evaluations with indifference, fear, or anger. Surveys are awkward assessments of teaching. One wants to "earn the appreciation of honest critics," as Ralph Waldo Emerson said. But with the anonymity granted by the typical evaluation questionnaire, it is hard to know which critics said what, and therefore what weight to give to the comments. Ultimately, survey criticism is rarely pleasant to receive. One can't reply to the critics. And institutional pressures or one's career situation can amplify the stress surrounding the evaluations. It is understandable then, that some instructors file evaluations away for viewing later or never.

There is, however, a positive argument for studying the evaluations. The feedback gives yet another opportunity to listen to the students. A capacity to *listen* is a hallmark of a strong teacher. Also, to be a professional is to commit oneself to steady growth in that field. For the sake of growth, one needs to read and think about the feedback from students. Student feedback with all its flaws can lead to good outcomes; but the instructor needs to approach it in the right way. Here are some tips on how to take stock of your classroom work at the end of a course.

Reading the tea leaves

First, write your own evaluation. You, after all, have an important perspective on how things went. Flip through your course syllabus, and jot down some notes about the course design, materials, and classroom teaching experience. Do this while the course is still fresh in your mind. Having your own assessment serves to frame the students' comments in a way that can offer insights: not just "good" versus "bad" but also the degree of alignment between you and the students. Misalignment can point toward improvements that may not be readily apparent in the student evaluations only.

Read the students' evaluations twice, the first time quickly to gain a sense of the whole. If the feedback is worse than you expected, catch your breath; put it aside for a while until you can reread it more objectively. If the feedback is complimentary, you have a different challenge, though no less important: find the humility to look for genuine opportunities for improvement. Re-read the evaluations slowly, and consider the following:

- **Cross-sectional patterns**: Student evaluations, in particular, are very noisy; the objective should be to find the signal rather than marinate in noise, or even add to it. There may be clusters of comments that point to a common behavior. Try to separate comments by focus of criticism: teaching versus materials versus course design. Note what seems to be going well, and should be continued. Too easily we focus on the criticisms without acknowledging successes. Sort students' qualitative written comments into two piles, positive and negative. Make separate inventories of each.

- **Command and connection.** Look for evidence of these critically important qualities. Their absence is a showstopper. "Command" is shorthand for confidence, authority in the subject, apparent mastery. Effective teachers seem to know what they talk about. Command also has an interpersonal dimension: the ability to gain the attention, respect, and following of students. "Connection" is shorthand for attending to the students: to know who they are, to listen well in and out of class, to understand the learning opportunities and challenges they face, to sense where they might be struggling, and simply to be available. As important as it is ungrammatical is the complaint that "the teacher don't hear so good." Lack of connection is not consistent with student centered teaching. Fortunately, issues of command and connection can be remedied. Numerous small tricks of the trade are helpful here, though often overlooked in the myopic belief offered by some that the material teaches itself. These tricks include arriving at class early, staying after class, being present at the student café during coffee breaks or at lunch—these having in common being where the students are.

- **Look at the details**. To a large extent the overall evaluation of your teaching is the least useful information in the feedback, for it says little about what you might do differently next time. The large results are built up from the details of your teaching. In this regard, the qualitative comments offered by students are valuable. You can do something about criticisms such as "Her handwriting on the chalkboard is too small," or "He only calls on students in the front row," or "The three class meetings on X left me utterly confused," or "The technical notes were riddled with typos."

- **Your norms versus theirs.** Many community norms are not discovered until violated. New teachers and visiting instructors are especially vulnerable to this. Examples might involve cold-calling, handing out solutions to cases, assigning a heavy workload on weekends, and requiring teamwork. In some schools these are expected; in others forbidden. The point here is that a close reading of the evaluations can help crystallize an understanding of school norms, your own philosophy of teaching, and where they collide.

- **Trends over time**. How does the most recent evaluation compare to earlier evaluations? Do the same comments tend to recur? What do these trends imply for your personal development agenda?

What is to be done?

Don't merely inventory the details of changes to be made. Rather, reflect on the process of developing your discussion leadership skills. These are always a work-in-progress.

- **Crystallize your priorities.** Think critically about what students seem to want you to change. Not all requests must be granted. One good criterion for assessing the implied requests is to ask *whether the change will promote better learning.* For instance, suppose you were criticized for routinely not ending class on time. You may choose not to change your practice in the belief that what really matters is how the learning comes together toward the end of class and that occasionally a punctual ending is worth sacrificing for solid learning.

- **Manage the feedback process.** End-of-course student surveys have their drawbacks. Consider gaining other points of reference, such as mid-course surveys, videotapes, and classroom observations by your colleagues. Informal conversation with one's own students can be very revealing. Given the alternative sources of feedback, it is a mistake to wait until the end of the course to find out how you are doing. A feeling of *surprise* at seeing the evaluations may be stark evidence that you don't listen well to the students or the classroom process.

- **Get an attitude—the *right* attitude.** Some novices worry that they don't have the instinct or charisma *ever* to get good evaluations. This flies in the face of abundant evidence and my own experience that the capacity to teach very well can be *learned*. You have a career as a teacher, of which this one recent course was a small episode. Resolve to learn from it, and grow to be a better teacher.

- **Be student centered, and trust that decent evaluations will follow.** Occasionally an instructor will try to teach in ways expressly designed to get good student evaluations. Such an attitude produces a bonfire of aberrant behavior, including under-targeted homework assignments, aggressive socializing with students, liberal distribution of "solutions" to the class discussions, and grade inflation. The underlying premises here are that campaigning works, and that challenging the students leads to bad evaluations. This may be true for some students. But in general students value instructors from whom they have *learned* well. This suggests that the straightest path to positive evaluations is to focus on learning, and the delivery of an intellectually valuable experience.

- **Accept variance.** Unfortunate feedback is the occasional companion of any instructor who takes risks with new material, tries new teaching styles, gets a poor draw of students, or believes that challenging students is good. You and your Deans should accept the prospect, and acknowledge that if one relentlessly gets *perfect* evaluations, one might not be trying hard enough.

- **Be action-oriented.** Focus on what you can do differently next time rather than what happened in the past. Distill what you have learned from the evaluations into a few important "to do's" rather than a detailed inventory of all possible improvements. These should be priorities in your personal development agenda for the coming year. They should have action steps beginning soon: reading on teaching techniques, asking to observe a successful colleague's class; asking a colleague to observe you at a few points during your course; searching for more suitable course materials; tinkering with the course design to put your best foot forward. Above all, don't shrink from the task. The care and attention to you give this season can pay huge dividends in the years to come.

Chapter 16
Mentoring Teachers

Of all the steps you might take to teach or learn the craft of discussion leadership, mentoring is one of the most difficult. But done well, I believe it is one of the most effective. To mentor and be mentored is to discuss in detailed, repeated, critical, and supportive fashion one's growth and tribulations as a case teacher. This should entail classroom observations by each person of the other, and should extend to discussing, in advance, preparations to teach an individual case, as well as the larger strategy underlying the course design. This is easy to describe, but challenging to implement. This chapter outlines some key attributes of successful mentoring offered mainly from the *standpoint of the mentor*. One can imagine a parallel set of comments for the colleague being mentored (whom I call the "learner"). I chose to adopt the mentor's perspective in order to help the novice teacher understand the challenges that one's mentor may confront, believing that this can help the learner engage a mentor more effectively. Consider therefore, these drivers of a successful mentoring experience:

1. **Engagement through chemistry and respect.** Mentoring simply by fiat is prone to fail. Each party has to want to engage the other. The mentor and learner need the positive chemistry that will tide them over frank conversations. Even more, they need to be motivated by respect for each other. The large implication of this is that Deans and other faculty leaders must move with the artifice of a matchmaker in hoping to start a mentoring process.

2. **School culture.** A mentoring process is probably not sustainable over the long run without strong support among the entire faculty and strong beliefs that it will and must occur for the good of the institution and the individual. It must be part of the expectations for accomplished teachers that their professional work should include this activity. It should be part of the implicit contract for novice teachers that they participate. Annual performance reviews should acknowledge efforts in a mentoring process. Faculty assignments to teaching teams should anticipate mentoring opportunities. It helps if the mentor is working in parallel on the same teaching challenges as the learner. This would occur, for instance, in teaching different sections of a large team-taught course. There, the mentor has a true incentive to replicate the learner's work in parallel, compare notes in real time (ideally, in advance of the class meetings), and debrief shortly thereafter.

3. **Warmth: care for the learner, and passion about the craft.** The best mentors manifestly care about both the craft and the learner. What mentors might need to say is not always pleasant, but it should be done in a way that preserves dignity for the learner and conveys esteem in which they hold him or her.[77]

4. **Make time, take time.** One of the clearest signals of caring is the regularity with which the mentor meets the learner. We are all busy. There are plenty of reasons to skip a meeting, or cut short the time, or wait for the learner to take all the initiative. For mentoring to succeed, it simply has to be as important as those other activities.

5. **Clarity about responsibility for results.** Learners will almost certainly fail in some respects. The mentor needs to encourage, reflect on problems, and perhaps brainstorm about solutions. But the mentor is not a fixer. The responsibility for results must be the learner's. In the book, *The Road Less Traveled*, the author, Scott Peck, recounted complaining about workload to his mentor. The mentor simply replied, "I agree, you have a problem," and left it for Peck to own up to the fact that he had created the problem by his own choices. Years after, Peck wrote, "We cannot solve a problem by hoping that someone else will solve it for us."

6. **Talk about specifics...but don't micromanage.** "God is in the details," said the architect, Mies van der Rohe. If the mentor focuses well on specifics, larger learnings will take care of themselves. See Chapter 14, "How to Observe a Colleague Teach a Case" for a way to generate specific discussion items. Note, however, that giving the learner specific, detailed instructions (e.g., "you must do it this way") actually undercuts learning. It gets in the way of the learner's ownership of success or failure. Micromanaging denies the learner the experience of translating any learning into action. It is by learning how to take action that the learner becomes a masterful teacher. Instead, encourage the learner with "have you tried...?"

7. **Talk from your own experience.** History may repeat itself. Your experience from yesterday may be relevant to a new teacher today. Acknowledge that you faced the same problem, and how you handled it. This legitimizes the experience for the learner and conveys many possible lessons: that the problem can be fixed; that accomplished teachers get into tough situations; that failure is not devastating; that risk-taking and innovation are useful.

---

[77] For an example of a mentor's care and encouragement, I recommend reading *Letters to a Young Poet* by Rainer Maria Rilke.

8. **Tell your truth.** The learner is ill served by "happy talk" that minimizes a problem. At the same time, easy does it--this is no place to inflict on another person the anger or resentment you may have accumulated under the sway of other mentors. The point of truth telling is not to preach, but to help the colleague grow.

9. **Build energy and enthusiasm for the discussion leadership craft.** Just as teachers draw energy from students, so students draw energy from teachers. Help the learner see your own passion for teaching.

10. **Be a learner too.** Consider not only what you bring to the discussion, but also what you can draw from it. A common misperception is that the mentor only gives, and the learner only takes. Mentors in those kinds of engagements tend to burn out quickly. The best combinations offer the mentor some opportunity to learn. Indeed, the mentor needs to enter the engagement with a mindset that the learner has something to teach. Similarly, the learner should look to bring insights to the mentor.

11. **In for a penny, in for a pound.** Once conversations begin about teaching, they may soon widen to associated issues regarding research, administrative duties, and general citizenship at the school. The mentor should be prepared to speak up as these other issues appear.

12. **Be sensitive to differences:** gender, age, seniority, race, etc. The aim should be to help the learner find a resonant teaching style consistent with his or her attributes, rather than to clone what works for the mentor. Differences in seniority are especially tricky—a tenured colleague advising an untenured colleague can inadvertently convey a variety of loaded messages about the learner's future in the profession.

The list could be extended. But the general conclusion from these dozen points is indicative of a more comprehensive discussion: mentoring a colleague is a costly and demanding process. One can think of other red flags too. Mentoring can fail to help. The benefits of mentoring may take long to appear. Moreover, mentoring is not the only determinant of teaching success—intelligence, experience, and formal training no doubt have an effect. Many colleagues feel ill equipped by training or temperament to be mentors. All these reasons explain, I believe, why so few schools try it.

To respond to these reservations, however, I offer my "pitch" for mentoring:

- I have seen it work decisively. Persuaded by the force of these examples, I am confident that it can really help where the school recruits teachers carefully and establishes the kind of serious program outlined here.

- Not mentoring is very costly as well. The faculty development approach of "toss 'em in, and see if they swim" assumes relatively low costs to faculty and students for failure in the classroom and low costs to the school for faculty recruitment and turnover. Teachers on the front line recognize the fallacies in these assumptions. These costs cannot be ignored; the pressures on business schools to improve teaching are rising. As Derek Bok said, "If you think education is expensive, try ignorance."

- Helping a colleague find his or her resonant style as a teacher is unusually satisfying. The mentor learns a great deal in the process. And much like other kinds of teaching, mentoring plants a legacy that will be harvested for years.

Take some time to consider the possible steps you personally, or your institution, might take to launch a mentoring effort.

Chapter 17
Digital-Friendly But Learning-Focused:
The Place of Technology

Being digital is the license to grow.
--Nicholas Negroponte[78]

Communications power doubles every six months.
--George Gilder[79]

The new information technology creates a race for teachers to adapt, cheered by students who value flexibility and novelty and by corporate partners who want their new recruits trained in the latest and greatest. However fleet of foot the instructor might be, the workout required to keep up with the pack is nontrivial. There is always new software or systems around the bend. The price tag for it all requires smelling salts for Deans. And though the invention and experimentation brings tangible rewards to teaching, it also carries unintended adverse side effects too. The finish line to this race keeps moving outward. And getting there successfully depends crucially on flexibility, a learning attitude, and *never* forgetting that all this should be done in the service of students.

The motive for going digital is to improve the teacher's *reach* and *richness* of contact with students. The interesting developments include:

- **Videoconference and webcasting.** Teachers can project themselves to other classrooms (or even the student's home) at great distances—this broadens their reach. It may also broaden the richness of student learning if the virtual learning community that is created contains helpful interaction among a diverse body of people.

- **Digital teaching materials.** These new materials range from simply digitizing the traditional printed case study to a case that is interactive and truly multi-media with text, video, animated graphics, and spreadsheets. These new materials can broaden the instructional reach by perhaps making them easier to access in distant

---

[78] Nicholas Negroponte, *Being Digital* New York: Vintage Books, 1995, page 41.
[79] George Gilder, *Telecosm: How Infinite Bandwidth Will Revolutionize Our World* New York: Free Press, 2000, page 265.

locations. And they deepen richness to the extent that the materials can contain valuable presentations not conveyed on the printed page.

- **Interactive tutorials.** Instructors know that a fraction of their students command a disproportionate share of time in the office, for what amounts to tutoring. These are students struggling to catch up or grasp an idea, usually through a process of discussing examples and looking for errors. Sometimes all the student wants is objective knowledge expressed in conversation. Information technology is well suited to handle tutorial work dealing with objective knowledge. Most of the major textbook publishers now offer separate CD-ROM tutorials in some aspect of one's course. These tutorials engage students in a very different way from simply reading a printed page. Many schools recommended these tutorials on an optional basis to students in their introductory finance courses. The anecdotal feedback from the students who use the tutorials is quite positive and suggests that they deepen student learning. They also afford help available on demand, thus effectively broadening the reach of the instructor.

- **Communication, distribution, sharing and polling.** Many instructors now see email as an indispensable means of reaching students, and responding to specific questions. Websites prove to be valuable repositories of resources for students. The Internet and email permit the instructor to survey student sentiment about a case or problem before, during, and after class.

Some colleagues meet developments like these with warm embrace, and others with horror and disgust. At most schools this divergence in reactions can be the starting point for a rich discussion about the future of teaching and the development of excellent teachers.

To participate effectively in these discussions, it helps immensely if one's own views are informed by an appreciation of the technology and its limitations. The recommended readings at the end of this chapter offer a reasonable survey. Be warned, however, books in this field age as rapidly as the technology changes.

One should augment any program of reading in this area with more direct observation and experimentation, in order to understand the issues:

- Invest some time in **simply learning** about digital media: how students and faculty use them; how well they work; what advances are expected in the near future.

- **Watch other instructors** use digital media. Find one or two pioneers at your school and ask to sit in on their classes. Visit other schools and learn how they use the technology.

- **Form a study group** of faculty and staff colleagues to discuss advances in the field. Meet regularly with readings distributed in advance.

- Simply **imagine** ways in which elements of digital technology might broaden your teaching reach or deepen your students' learning. Then look for systems or software that meet your imagination. If none exist, consider inventing them.

- **Experiment.** If you have not done it before (and if your school has the equipment) try in-class videoconferencing with an executive or knowledgeable industry observer, related to a case or series of case discussions. Try teaching a digital case. Set up a course website.

- **Get close to your school's technical support people and their leaders.** Informal conversations well in advance of an experiment on your part can often help marshal the technical resources of an institution in fresh and useful ways. Anyway, pioneering experiments are always stressful; having a safety net of technical experts can make a huge difference.

The new technology is growing in usefulness and impact, but each of these new media creates fresh challenges for the instructor. Virtually every instructor who has experimented with digital media can relate one or two stories of technology run amok. But the broad mass of downside examples falls in the range of more mundane trials of patience.

Whether or not you choose to become a digital pioneer, the digital world is probably already entering your classroom in surprisingly distracting ways. Plagiarism from Internet resources is on the rise. Through email, students can feed each other discussion points that can help a student look good to the instructor, whether merited or not. Students can lose focus on the essential learning points of a class and turn attention to websurfing, emailing, or playing games. Increasingly one finds the interruption of a cellular phone call during class (despite requests to turn these off.) Instructors, too, can lose focus by becoming so enamored of the medium and its charms that they underdeliver on content. Common to all of these is a defection toward the trivial and away from learning and student growth.

Suppress any Luddite tendencies these frustrations may cause. Excellence in teaching invites us to be pioneers and experimenters, but with care and purpose about what happens in the classroom:

1. **Set expectations; express them clearly.** Added to the usual ground-rules to be surveyed at the start of a course, the instructor should be prepared to state (orally and in the syllabus) clear expectations about the sharing of digital resources among students (such as spreadsheets), clear attribution of the work of others obtained from the Internet, and the use of email and the web during class. Explain the limits in terms that appeal to maximizing the common good: the quality of learning and of the daily class discussions.

2. **Set an example.** Behave consistently with your own expectations of the students. As a general rule avoid taking communications during class (either cellular phone calls, emails, or handwritten notes).

3. **Manage the infrastructure; turn off the net in class.** This is quite effective, especially as a signal about your expectations. But it is at best a temporary solution as new wireless communication technologies arrive to circumvent the landwire systems.

4. **Manage the discussion-dampening impact of visual technology.** As with the old technology of overhead projectors, beaming up a PowerPoint lecture strangles discussion. If the use of projected material is unavoidable, keep it short, and pepper students with questions to stimulate their engagement with the projected material.

5. **Respond to digital behavior that detracts from learning.** Remaining silent is no strategy at all. You must be your own best champion of the quality of the learning experience.

6. **Work to build a school-wide culture that is both digital-friendly and learning-focused.** Set norms around which a school community can rally, rather than course-specific rules that students will chip away. Enlist the support of other faculty and the Dean for a set of common expectations of behavior. Technology bashing is a tone to avoid: the fundamental issue here is the quality of learning.

7. **Stay close to students**; the next technology surprise is just around the corner. Don't assume that once you have fixed the current problem, it is fixed for good. Instead, ask continually how the digital revolution can both help and undermine the learning in one's classroom. Most importantly, the new technology will shape student attitudes about their expectations of the educational experience. For

instance, the concept of "always on"[80] may raise expectations about the availability of instructors and resources. IT infrastructure must become bulletproof to the kinds of interruptions that five or ten years ago one accepted. And finally, students are bound to seek more *modular* availability of learning experience; the ability to mix-and-match to give the student more choice and to meet the student where he or she is at present.

Obtaining and maintaining skills for excellent teaching require one not merely to adapt as the digital future unfolds but also to lead. One of the defining qualities of a leader is clarity about ultimate ends. However attractive and compelling the digital future is, it is also uncertain. Decades before the digital revolution, T.S. Eliot foresaw the competition among wisdom, knowledge, and information. He asked,

> *Where is the wisdom we have lost in knowledge?*
> *Where is the knowledge we have lost in information?*[81]

These questions remain relevant for the student-centered teacher. Mere data can overwhelm knowledge. And knowledge can obscure wisdom. Yet it is growth in wisdom that we should want most to promote. There is probably a digital path toward wisdom, though it largely remains to be discovered. I encourage the discussion leader to proceed with the discovery process.

Appendix: Reading Suggestions

Being Digital by Nicholas Negroponte and *Telecosm* by George Gilder offer an articulate and buoyant advocacy of the need for organizations and their leaders to grow with the new technology. Their somewhat breathless and emphatic language can both inspire and repel. But keep an open mind.

E-learning by Marc J. Rosenberg[82] surveys digital approaches to instruction, mainly in the setting of corporations and professional firms. The applications he describes are

---

[80] "Always on" describes a computer that is always turned on and connected to the Internet. This suggests a resource that is always *immediately available* to the student or teacher without the time-consuming task of booting up the machine or connecting to the net. It also refers to always *receptive* to messages or new applications. Ultimately, the phrase suggests steady engagement with the digital world.

[81] T.S. Eliot, "Choruses from the Rock," *Collected Poems: 1909-1962*, New York: Harcourt Brace and World, 1963, page 147.

[82] Marc J. Rosenberg, *e-Learning*, New York: McGraw-Hill, 2001.

impressive, as are the cost advantages for employers. He discusses possible barriers to effective use of e-learning systems and what organizations might do to overcome them.

For leavening, one should read Clifford Stoll's *High-Tech Heretic: Reflections of a Computer Contrarian.*[83] Stoll skewers grossly inflated claims of technology enthusiasts. He argues that technology should get out of the way and make life easier and learning better for students. He does not explain why, if digital learning is deficient, firms and intelligent people are drawn to it, though by the end of the book the answer is fairly clear: digital technology is excellent for transmitting objective knowledge, while genuine learning is much more elusive. Still, Stoll's book remains an important cautionary admonition to the digital instructor.

Learnativity.com, a website maintained by Marcia Conner, is the best-in-class Internet resource on digital learning. Neither a techno-enthusiast nor a Luddite, she offers a realistic perspective. She writes, "With good design and delivery, eLearning does [a number of good] things. But, at its heart, it is, simply, learning. Too bad most interpretations focus on the technology (the "e") and not on the learning." She also offers an up-to-date list of technology-related and student-focused books.

The Social Life of Information by John Seely Brown and Paul Duguid[84] sheds valuable light on the social limitations of digital technology. They offer an assessment of the promise of information technology for society that acknowledges a distinction among Eliot's wisdom, knowledge, and information. Chapter 5 of their book discusses the difference between objective and tacit knowledge, and between "know how" and "know that." If one wants to produce graduates who will be effective practitioners, then one must teach a fair amount of tacit knowledge, and "know how." Learning this kind of knowledge requires a social process, and "networks of practice." The computer and advanced telecommunications can either help or hinder the formation of such networks by the student. They conclude,

> *One reason knowledge may be so hard to give and receive is that knowledge seems to require more by way of assimilation. Knowledge is something we digest rather than merely hold. It entails the knower's understanding and some degree of commitment. ...So learning, the*

---

[83] Clifford Stoll, *High-Tech Heretic: Reflections of a Computer Contrarian*, New York: Anchor Books, 1999.
[84] John Seely Brown and Paul Duguid, *The Social Life of Information* Boston: Harvard Business School Press, 2000.

acquisition of knowledge, presents knowledge management with its central challenge.[85]

Brown and Duguid critique the conventional wisdom that new technology will disaggregate educational institutions, demassify consumption, and disintermediate students and knowledge, causing the demise of physical universities, and the rise of the virtual. They write,

> *Learners need three things from an institution of higher education: access to authentic communities of learning, interpretation, exploration, and knowledge creation; resources to help them work with both distal and local communities; and widely accepted representations for learning and work. Change in the system still needs to honor those constraints.*[86]

---

[85] Brown and Duguid, *ibid.*, p. 120.
[86] Brown and Duguid, *ibid.* p. 232.

Chapter 18
The Teaching Portfolio:
A Device for Refining and Communicating
Your Work in the Classroom

Mark Twain barely contained his use of profanity, a problem his wife abhorred and sought to cure. One evening, he and she were dressing for a formal dinner when a button popped off his shirt. He launched a tirade against buttons, formal shirts, and evening wear. After a few minutes, the profanity subsided. Twain's wife decided to use the moment to remind her husband to govern his language. Calmly, and in a flat voice, she repeated, word for word, the entire tirade. Twain replied, "It would pain me to think that when I swear it sounds like that. You got the words right, Livy, but you don't know the tune."[87]

Much the same could be said of the way scholars describe their teaching. The typical curriculum vitae emphasizes written work over teaching. Promotion portfolios usually consist of a solid discussion of the candidate's intellectual contribution as a researcher, combined with a simple list of courses taught and perhaps some teaching ratings. The presentation has some words about teaching, but none of the music: choices made in course design; risks taken; successes (or learnings from failures); teaching philosophy and style; interpretation of the teaching ratings; growth as a teacher and plans for continued professional development. Absent these, the presentation of one's teaching is like the language of Twain's wife, flat and tuneless.

Teaching should not be the hidden dimension in a summary of professional work. In virtually all schools, the quality of teaching is a priority. Pressure from students, recruiters, donors, and within school faculties has elevated the need for exemplary teaching. In addition, teaching competence in all its manifestations absorbs an enormous part of professional time and energy. To ignore it is to deny a large chunk of one's professional life. Ultimately, this kind of denial can create a self-fulfilling prophecy; if one's teaching isn't important enough to discuss and be proud of, it can wither.

A teaching portfolio, a 5-10 page document along with appendices and supplements, should describe the teaching dimension of one's professional work. Specifically, it surveys teaching assignments, philosophy, style, accomplishments, innovations, and

---

[87] Quoted from Albert Bigelow Paine's authorized biography, *Mark Twain*, 1912, page 559.

evidence of teaching effectiveness. Rather like the professional portfolio of an artist, composer, or writer, the teaching portfolio shows your best work and perhaps argues for better work to come.

The concept of the teaching portfolio

The teaching portfolio is an *evidence-based* document about one's teaching philosophy and effectiveness. It is a compilation of reflections and work to indicate a teaching trajectory. The portfolio is necessarily a mixture of documentation and advocacy —one is framing the past work as a teacher, but doing so in a fact-based way.

The teaching portfolio complements professional summations of one's research, administrative service, consulting or government service, and outreach. Thus, the teaching portfolio would serve easily as a segment of one's entire professional portfolio.

The term, "portfolio," has two senses: (a) a 6-10 page narrative that presents an overview and summary of teaching work; and (b) the narrative *and* supporting appendices which together might fill a large three-ring binder. The discussion that follows focuses on the narrative only since completing the narrative is the entry barrier to the larger work. Needless to say, a finished job should include narrative and appendices.

Why prepare it?

There are numerous possible motives for presenting one's professional work as a teacher:

- **Entering the job market.** Many newly minted Ph.D.s have taught and wish to present themselves to the market as accomplished classroom leaders.

- **Prepare for tenure and promotion decisions.** Candidates want, and need, to discuss their teaching. Promotion committees place increasing emphasis on teaching skills. Discussion of the candidate's past experience and plans in this area addresses a large swath of work.

- **Document good work done; leave a legacy.** Instructors who are cycling out of challenging teaching assignments will find the portfolio an excellent device for conveying learnings and suggestions to the inbound instructors. Senior colleagues carry a wealth of tacit knowledge that if captured in a portfolio can strengthen the efforts of their junior colleagues.

- **Get perspective; take stock.** The teaching portfolio is an excellent vehicle for reflecting on where one has been and is headed in one's development as a teacher.

- **Contribute to a conversation about teaching philosophy and style.** Within any school resides a variety of philosophies and approaches. A collection of teaching portfolios can help make that variety transparent and the basis for a richer discussion about teaching within the school.

What it contains

No formal template exists for the teaching portfolio. The contents are necessarily idiosyncratic. The document must be adapted to the attributes of the writer and the purposes of the portfolio. To stimulate the reader's imagination, here is a list of elements one might consider including in the portfolio:

1. **Introduction:** why you are writing this, and what the narrative contains.

2. **A summary of your teaching.** This should include course titles, years, numbers of students, and references to course syllabuses given in an appendix. The survey should also refer to all the ways in which one "teaches": responsibilities for delivering courses in degree programs, advising students and projects, supervising Ph.D. candidates, leading educational programs, teaching in non-degree programs, teaching in private consulting.

3. **A description of how you teach.** This gives a profile of your teaching style. What is a "typical" class of yours like? How do you prepare? How do you implement your plans? What do you find easy? Challenging? Done thoughtfully, this section should paint an engaging picture of your work in the classroom.

4. **A statement of why you teach that way and your teaching philosophy.** This illuminates your values and concept of exemplary teaching.

5. **A discussion of the linkage** between your teaching, research, and service to the school. Common to many successful professionals is connectivity or integration among one's work activities. You might discuss how your research and service inform, enrich, and energize your teaching.

6. **Highlighted examples** of your teaching efforts. Your "best hits" should be profiled here. You might survey a successful course design (with syllabus), an educational program you delivered, teaching materials you prepared, and/or an

illustration of how your teaching style adapted to new circumstances or challenges.

7. **Evidence of your teaching effectiveness.** Most schools prepare numerical evaluations of instructors and give benchmark ratings for the entire faculty against which your evaluations can be compared. But you can go farther, quoting from a sample of students' qualitative comments that highlight your particular strengths, or from unsolicited (and perhaps solicited) letters and emails that comment on your teaching effectiveness. Finally, you might incorporate examples of outstanding student work[88] done under your direction, with a commentary by you showing how this work reflects your teaching.

8. **Plans for continuing professional development.** What skills would you like to learn, or develop further? How will you pursue these? Your discussion here might reference activities such as a program of reading, classroom observation (of you and by you), videotaping, and attending workshops and presentations.

The list could be extended considerably. The reader will find suggestions for more items in the resources recommended at the end of this document.

How to prepare a portfolio

While there are no "correct" models for the teaching portfolio, there are probably many wrong ones. The following tips are aimed at avoiding some common problems, and simply completing the job:

- **Obtain a clear sense of audience to strike the right tone.** The tone of the portfolio will vary in subtle ways from one audience to the next. In some instances (such as a candidacy for tenure) one should solicit advice about the contents of the document.

- **Study exemplars.** Some universities maintain collections of teaching portfolios. For instance, the University of Virginia maintains a collection of portfolios at the Teaching Resource Center (see the recommended resources listed at the end of this chapter).

---

[88] The writer should *always* solicit the permission of students to include their work in the portfolio, copy it, or place it on the web.

- **Attend a teaching portfolio workshop.** Some universities offer short programs in which participants collaborate in the development of teaching portfolios. Comments, suggestions, and coaching in these settings can be invaluable.

- **Get a portfolio mentor.** This should be a sympathetic individual who understands the nature of your writing challenge and is a critical thinker. Experience suggests that mentors outside of one's own discipline are more helpful than those closer to home.

- **Be careful not to undersell; don't be afraid to crow.** The portfolio should contain one's best work. Some achievements may not speak for themselves; elaborate a little for the reader.

- **Avoid overblown, unsupported language.** This is a constraint on the preceding point. Try carefully to document assertions, especially those about teaching effectiveness. Don't get carried away in presenting your work. Use simple declarative sentences.

- **Focus the discussion in the document around just a few key ideas; avoid a collection of random statements.** Step into the shoes of the reader and ask, "What is this person trying to say?" Most people are selective readers. Long, unfocused documents risk muddying what may be a central message.

- **Avoid redundancy.** You can overcompensate in trying to drive home a central message.

- **Keep the narrative short, to a maximum of 10 typewritten pages.** It is easy to write a long, unfocused narrative, and hard to achieve focus and brevity. Provide adequate time to refine the document.

Though these points are common sense for all writing, they have special importance in the case of the teaching portfolio. One is rarely trained in the development of these documents; reminders like these will help.

The best advice in writing a portfolio is to keep one's attention on ultimate aims. The point of the effort is not to write a portfolio, but rather to accomplish something else, such as to get a job, become a better teacher, or remind yourself and others of all you have done.

Recommended resources for further study

UVa's Teaching Resource Center maintains an excellent collection of written materials on the subject of the teaching portfolio. Visit the TRC at http://trc.virginia.edu/. University of Virginia, Teaching Resource Center, Hotel D, 24 East Range, P.O. Box 400136, Charlottesville, Virginia 22904-4136, telephone 434-982-2815.

Murray, John P., *Successful Faculty Development and Evaluation: The Complete Teaching Portfolio*, ASHE-ERIC Higher Education Report No. 8. Washington, D.C.: The George Washington University, Graduate School of Education and Human Development, 1995.

Schoenfeld, A. Clay, and Robert Magnan, *Mentor in a Manual: Climbing the Academic Ladder to Tenure*, 2nd ed., Madison, WI: Magna, 1994. See especially the chapter, "Documenting your Teaching Activities," pages 254-258.

Seldin, Peter, *The Teaching Portfolio: A practical guide to improved performance and promotion/tenure decisions*, 2nd ed., Bolton MA: Anker Publishing Company, Inc. ISBN 1-882982-150-0. The first two chapters of this book may be viewed on the Internet at the following address:
http://www.lgu.ac.uk/deliberations/portfolios/ICED_workshop/seldin_book.html.

Seldin, P., Annis, L, and Zbizarreta, J., (1995) "Answers to common questions about the teaching portfolio," *Journal on Excellence in College Teaching*, 6(1), 57-64.

Sample teaching portfolios on the Web

http://trc.virginia.edu//barnett/
http://www.people.virginia.edu/~cd4y/
http://curry.edschool.virginia.edu/curry/class/edlf/589_004/
http://faculty.darden.edu/brunerb/resources.htm

Part 4
Shaping the Learning Experience

Overview

This section considers the element of *design* in helping to create effective learning. As the word, "shaping," suggests, the design aspect may be more like sculpture than engineering. The design choices span many dimensions:

- The **course** design (Chapter 19).

- The design of individual **class** meetings through choices about questions and assignments (Chapter 20).

- The use of **repetition** with and across individual class meetings (Chapter 21).

- The use and support of **student teamwork** (Chapter 22).

- **Opening a course** (Chapter 23) and shaping student expectations (Chapter 24).

- **Visualizing** the path of discussion, and using concepts of *contagion* to stimulate energy in discussions (Chapter 25).

- Managing **toughness and demands** on students (Chapter 26).

- Drawing the learning experience to a **close** (Chapter 27).

- **Grading** and the conveyance of feedback to the student (Chapter 28).

Chapter 19
Designing a Case-Method Course and Communicating the Design to Students

In Maine, the story is told of two villagers at a county fair who won a raffle to ride in a balloon. They climbed into the basket, released the mooring line, and sailed into the sky. Soon they drifted into a cloudbank and lost sight of land for some time. Eventually, the sky cleared enough for them to spy land, and see a farmer working in a field. They let some of the gas out of the balloon, and slowly descended. "Where are we?" they called to the farmer. "You're in a balloon, you damn fools," he replied.

To identify your location, it helps for the guide—the instructor—to have the "satellite photo" in mind and to communicate it in various ways in order to stimulate the process of discovery. The most successful discussion-method courses have in common many of the following attributes:

- **Focus on learning, not teaching.** The first rule in the design of a course is to start where the student starts. Define the student and his or her needs. From their starting point, construct the required understanding. Use "bottom-up" design.

- **A Few "Big Ideas."** A large temptation of a teacher is to cover many ideas in the belief that this adds the most value to the student. But this focuses on volume instead of quality and ignores the basic fact that repetition is one of the soundest foundations of learning. In the pursuit of adding extra value to the student, an emphasis on quality of learning (rather than quantity) must rule. One must ask, "What few big ideas, which, if learned well, will make this course truly valuable?" The answer should become the underlying themes of the course. The instructor can return to these ideas repeatedly and use them to shape the closure for the students. These are the kinds of ideas that students will recall for a long time.

- **Conceptual or Topical Flow:** A good course design has a beginning, middle, and end; it *flows*. An important benefit of a good design is that it fosters the students' trust and respect for the instructor, which can yield huge dividends when the time comes to convey difficult concepts or techniques. More importantly, if topics are structured on top of each other, each new module of cases reinforces the work in earlier modules; the learning gain is multiplicative rather than merely additive. Working against flow are a number of forces: the temptation to be eclectic, a list of favorite teaching materials, the absence of good materials on particular topics, the natural reluctance to dally with new and uncertain teaching materials, the belief that the students are responsible for figuring things out for themselves; and the awkwardness with which most subjects fit into a linear course plan. Fight these. A way to begin the process of building the flow of your course is to survey the materials available and to look for ways in which they fit well together. One strives to build a mosaic of individual learning experiences in which the individual pieces fit with, and contribute to a sensible whole.

- **Carefully Designed Beginnings and Endings:** The opening and closing of a course (and of modules within it) present excellent opportunities to frame the subject matter of the course. At the opening, one creates expectations about the contents of the course and the effort necessary to absorb the contents. Above all, the course opener should convey some of the intellectual excitement inherent in your subject. At the closing, one has the opportunity to summarize and build students' self-confidence in mastery of the material. I like to use comprehensive cases to open the course. There, the challenge for the student is to assess a situation rather than to crunch numbers—assessment permits students to focus on themes rather than on minute details. Comprehensive cases also challenge the students from the outset. Many instructors prefer the opposite opening strategy. They use a relatively simple case, seeking to minimize possible confusion at the start of the course and to give even novices a sense of accomplishment on the opening day. At the close of a course, comprehensive cases help review the terrain covered by the course and build student confidence.

- **Variety in Delivery:** Variety enlivens student participation and learning. Within a course, an instructor can achieve considerable variety along the following dimensions:

Format: A steady stream of standard case discussions can be leavened with classes based on team presentations, role-plays, or negotiation exercises.

Task: Students appreciate a mixture of both basic analytic problems and situations in which interpretation and the exercise of managerial judgment are important.

Pacing/Intensity: Try to offer a mixture of cases according to challenge. Students welcome periodic "breathers" and opportunities to dwell more carefully than usual on a complex situation. Other cases are rich enough to be taught over two class periods if time permits detailed exploration.

Direction/Ambiguity: Another dimension of variation is the degree to which the instructor "sets up" the case discussion—that is, through a choice of problem or use of advance assignment questions. For instance, my own book of case studies contains a number of relatively ambiguous, less directive cases that are useful vehicles for problem identification, for which the case method is excellent exercise.

Variation of unknowns: An instructor tries to reinforce what has come before without being repetitious. It may help to have one day's case solve for B given A, and the next day's case solve for A given B.

- **Helping the Students Help Themselves:** In the case method, one often observes that the hardest-won insights are the best learned. Unfortunately, this kind of "best learning" is difficult to stimulate: the instructor must walk a thin line between giving away too much and giving away too little. Ultimately, I believe the best an instructor can do is to help prepare students for the process of self-discovery in the following ways:

Collateral readings: Where especially useful, a day's assignment may recommend articles and textbook chapters that help set the conceptual foundations for the case analysis. Habitually assigning supporting readings, however, might signal to the student that the case is an extended problem meant to exercise a specific technique in the reading, which no true case study will do effectively.

Course tracking: Preparing a syllabus and sending periodic memos to students can help them track the flow of the course and follow the progressive structure of concepts and techniques. Memos should not present case solutions but should remind students about ideas/techniques/terms recently presented and worth thinking about further. One caution to the use of these memos is that they may become available to subsequent classes of students through fraternity course folders—thus be careful not to "solve" the cases for your students through these memos.

Study Groups: Small group discussions before class can be an extremely effective device for building self-confidence and student mastery of the material. The instructor can encourage the voluntary formation of these groups simply by suggesting the idea and letting motivated individuals do the rest. In my experience, a significant percentage of students will participate in study groups. (Incidentally, when study groups are used, the instructor will need to establish the norm that every student is individually accountable for class preparation; one needs to discourage free riding.)

Feedback: Quizzes, exams, and written and oral comments on class contribution can give students a sense of their grasp of the material and can motivate students' efforts to consolidate course material periodically.

- **Experimentation and tinkering.** The best case-method course designs grow out of relentless tinkering. Use case studies in whatever combinations make sense to you (i.e., rather than what case writers may advise). Students genuinely respect instructors who are themselves seekers and learners. Yet all too often instructors rest on the laurels of a successful course design ("If it ain't broke, don't 'fix' it.") or resist the professional exposure of trying new course designs and materials ("It ain't in my paycheck.") To these one can reply:

> *"Success is never final."* These immortal words of Winston Churchill have borne the test of time in both politics and business. Typically, an industry leader will neglect product or process improvements and then decline. In like manner, course designs gradually grow stale. To prevent this, one must continually tinker.

> *"A mistake is an event, the full benefit of which has not yet been turned to your advantage."* (Edwin Land, founder of Polaroid.) One runs risks by tinkering with course designs. Often they pay off handsomely. But the occasional failures need to be viewed as failed lab experiments--the source of insights on which to build the next success.

Karl Weick argued that true teaching was itself a learning process for the instructor, a philosophy that carries important implications for course design:

When teaching becomes learning, then once something is learned, it is time to move on to something else. Each year, I throw away most of my lecture notes, syllabi, and exercises. And each year I vow never to do that again. And each year I build most of my courses from scratch. This makes it tough to build a reputation for a course because, whatever new students expect on the basis of previous students, they seldom find. ...I believe strongly that there are such things as classics...yet I often act like a hypocrite. In the interest of learning, I treat nothing as classic...And I'm eternally on the lookout for unexpected classics...But even classics disappear for a year or so, only to reappear mysteriously and seemingly at random. What is constant amid all this shuffling is learning in real time.[89]

---

[89] In Karl E. Weick, "Teaching as Learning in Public," in *Researchers Hooked on Teaching*, Rae Andre and Peter J. Frost eds., Thousand Oaks, CA: Sage Publications, 1997, pages 294-295.

- **Communicating your design.** The final important element in any course design is a strategy for communicating the design to students. Remember the story of the balloonists: they *know* they're in a balloon, but have no idea of larger location. This is the predicament of many students. Self-discovery and making personal meaning out of a course are fundamental precepts of Socratic teaching, but well-timed communication about the direction and velocity of the course can help students find their own coordinates. The instructor has several tools to choose from in this regard:

  o **Course syllabus.** A carefully prepared syllabus is vital. Not only does it offer a general idea about the flow of a course, but in summarizing the grading, course requirements, and teacher's expectations, it forms the basis for the implicit contract between teacher and student. A number of faculty now place their course syllabi on the Internet.[90]

  o **Course web page.** The instructor can post a running commentary on the course here, together with any supplemental resources that will help students get their bearings. Included could be a "Frequently Asked Questions" (FAQ) department—these help forestall heavy office visits related to challenging aspects of the course.

  o **Module notes.** The instructor could distribute brief (e.g. 2-page) commentaries at the end of each general subject segment of the course. A module note should never give solutions or answers to cases but rather suggest linkages among the daily learning experiences.

  o **Class comments.** The instructor might use the opening and closing segments of class to comment on the direction of the course, the subjects, and next steps. Students could be invited to offer linkages among individual case discussions.[91]

Conclusion

In the aggregate, these eight pointers amount to viewing course design as *process* not product. If one continually asks the questions behind these pointers, effective designs will emerge.

---

[90] For examples of good use of web sites to present courses, see the sites of Campbell Harvey at Duke (http://www.duke.edu/~charvey/) and William Goetzmann at Yale (http://viking.som.yale.edu/).

[91] See my discussion of daily "Ahas" in chapter 20, "Repetition is the first principle of all learning."

Chapter 20
Designing a Case Method Teaching Plan

"**plan** v.t. To bother about the best method of accomplishing an accidental result."
-- Ambrose Bierce *The Devil's Dictionary*[92]

The discussion method educates best when it is student centered rather than instructor centered. Some discussion method teachers recognize this truth and, minimize their planning for individual classes. You hear some discussion leaders say, "Don't worry, the material teaches itself." I have seen these minimalist teaching plans end in both stunning success and bitter failure. The outcome is often driven by the existence of a view about the material and one's skills in active listening and discussion leadership.

If great outcomes are driven by views and skills, why should one plan? First and foremost, a plan imposes a discipline on one's own preparation of a case. Anticipating specific topics of discussion helps target your analysis effectively. Second, a plan can help anticipate areas of difficulty for the students. And third, the plan can serve as a compass for more active discussion leadership if the students' momentum loses its steam.

From the perspective of the student-centered teacher, *the teaching plan is not a script*. I draw on suggested teaching plans and depart from them freely, as the needs of the students and my own teaching goals required. Moreover, any time I teach a case, I tailor the teaching plan in ways suggested by the following questions:

- **Whom am I teaching?** What are their goals? Needs? Skills? An assessment of the course client is the origin of any plan. For instance, MBA students generally have an appetite for learning hard skills and conceptual frameworks. Business executives, on the other hand tend to want practical solutions to problems they encounter.

- **What are my teaching objectives in this session?** Why is this case in the course? Many of the cases in this book are rich enough to carry many teaching points. The relevant task of teaching is not maximization, however, but optimization. Shoehorning in all possible teaching points is less desirable than making a lasting impression of a few key points. The selection of specific teaching objectives should be dictated by the needs of the students and the

---

[92] Ambrose Bierce, *The Devil's Dictionary* New York: Oxford University Press, 1999, page 146.

conceptual flow of the course. The success of subsequent cases may depend on consolidation of earlier teaching points or the introduction of new ideas or both.

- **What question or statement is the most effective way to open the discussion?** I believe this question is the most difficult to answer in developing a teaching plan. A good opener sets the stage, raises the curtain effectively, and builds drama. Bad openers mire the discussion in trivial issues or issues that are substantive but far afield from the objectives of the discussion. The opener should be tailored to the nature of the case: where the case problem is clearly defined and specific figure analysis is to be done, I favor openers that help establish the relevance of the analysis and launch the discussion into the figures. For cases where the challenge is to define the problem, I favor openers that bring out the richness and complexity of the situation. An example of a good opener would be "What are the problems in this case? And what are your recommendations?" Another is "Who is the decision-maker here? And what must he or she be worried about?" An opener to avoid is, "What is the concept of XYZ, and what does the textbook tell us about it?"—this saps all engagement with a case problem.

- **What questions lead to breakthrough "Ahas"?** The middle of the discussion is the synthesis of facts and insights that leads to genuine learning. Random questioning can send a discussion far off course. Like the opener, questions for the body of the case discussion should be motivated by the teaching objectives of the case and the needs of the students. For instance, it may be useful to ask students to define new concepts or technical terms that may have surfaced. Also, the use of new forms of analysis could be explored as a foundation to understanding the usefulness of the resulting insights.

- **How should I close the discussion?** Some instructors believe that closure (in the form of class consensus or summary of teaching points) is unnecessary. What matters to them is the process of debate that occurred in the body of the case discussion. I prefer a formal closure as a way of concluding any drama that may have been created during the discussion. As the teaching plans in this manual show, one can use devices such as a vote of the class on a decision, the presentation of the epilogue to the case, or a discussion of summary points by either the students or the instructor. Used in this way, the closing is a learning opportunity for the students; indeed, the sharp reversals from expectations in some of the epilogues often leave the most lasting impressions of a case discussion.

- **How can I accommodate the "accident" of learning?** To students in the discussion method classroom, Ambrose Bierce seems correct: learning appears to be accidental. The discussion meanders. The class may work hard, only to turn around at the end of a blind alley. Then, almost by surprise, the discussion gathers momentum, and reaches a key destination. (For more on this, see Chapter 25, "Helping Discussions to Catch Fire.") In short, from the perspective of student and instructor, the discussion is hardly a direct path to insights. Yet the indirect path *is* where *learning* occurs. The teaching plans of great discussion leaders provide for the meandering, turnarounds, changes in momentum, and surprising arrivals. My colleagues Sherwood Frey and James Clawson argue that one can arrive at a decision using a number of different paths. Therefore, the task of the instructor is to anticipate the range of paths, and prepare a strategy of questioning that is flexible to the accidental discussion choices that students may make.

As these questions suggest, the instructor needs to manage the contradiction of two goods: flexibility and control. The choice of daily teaching objectives and of questions must spring from the instructor's view about the subject matter—the instructor must have a view. Yet at the same time, the plan must allow for student-centered exploration of the discussion problem. Chapter 27, "Gaining Closure," offers more discussion on managing this contradiction. The questions offered in this chapter lend a foundation for customizing your own student centered teaching plan.

Chapter 21
Repetition is the First Principle of All Learning

We shall not cease from exploration
And the end of all our exploring
Will be to arrive where we started
And know the place for the first time
                                    - T.S. Eliot
                                    The Dry Salvages

The deepest "ahas" spring from an encounter and then a return. Repeating the encounter fuses it into one's awareness. One of the biggest mistakes a teacher can make is to forego the return or repetition. The learning process is one of slow engagement with ideas; gradually the engagement builds to a critical mass when the student actually acquires the idea. Repetition matters because it can hasten and deepen the engagement process. If one cares about quality of learning, one should consciously design repetitive engagement into courses and daily teaching. Repetition is a valuable foundation for learning, across the most basic terms and definitions to the most sublime insights. To repeat well is harder than it seems.

A decade ago a friend and colleague said, "Repetition is the first principle of all teaching." I thought he was kidding, for it seemed to me then that there were many other better First Principles: mastery of the material, passion for the subject, empathy for the learning process, energy, and love of student interaction. But he was actually quite serious. He challenged me to think of all the ways in which I had learned because someone had restated or revisited a concept that I thought I had learned, but which yielded a deeper meaning in the new context. Then it struck me that repetition was primarily important to *learning*, rather than teaching. If one adopts a student-centered teaching approach, repetition will be a very important tactic for enhancing learning.

Over the intervening decade, my friend's words have returned to me in discussions about teaching and course design. Like the protagonist in the movie, *Groundhog Day*, I seemed fated to relive a conversation relentlessly. I discovered the importance of repetition, and the challenges of implementing repetition in a student centered way. However, teachers and program designers are caught between growth in content and the fixed or declining program time available. Virtually all educational programs are striving to cover more content in less time. Professionals and students are impatient to get trained quickly. In short, repetition seems in retreat.

The case to be made for building repetition into your teaching is that it supports a number of highly important educational goods: self-paced discovery, ability to reflect, consistency and clarity of thought--these promote deep learning. I learned that repetition works precisely because it provides a chance to reflect and remind a student, even if he or she ignored it in the first place. Done well, repetition is student centered. Of course, too much repetition has a dark side: boredom, student passivity, rote learning, and a high opportunity cost--one could be extending the reach of students into new areas instead of revisiting the old. The teacher needs to find the Goldilocks outcome, neither too much nor too little repetition.

The way to achieve a sensible balance is to start with a focus on learning rather than teaching; on the student rather than the teacher; on the ideas rather than the material. From this new perspective, repetition becomes a tactic to help the student self-teach ideas.

First, think of the variety of time frames in which to repeat an idea:

- **An individual class session.** One can use openings, middles and summaries to repeat ideas. As the saying goes, tell them what you're going to tell them, then tell them, then tell them what you told them—the unattractive aspect of this saying is that with all the telling, you're not doing much asking. Look for ways to repeat through asking.

- **A module of classes within a course.** Modules are the real building blocks of the repetitive cycle. One can start a module with an easy case that sketches the framework. Then one can gradually deepen students' grasp with successively richer cases.

- **Across an entire course.** At the opening of the course, one can plant ideas or themes that will be revisited at a number of points throughout the course and then become the framework for the crescendo at the close of the course.

- **Across a multi-course program.** Courses can, and should, support one another by visiting key ideas. A marketing course might use net present value to assess a strategy. A finance course might teach net present value with attention to marketing strategy as a value driver. Increasingly, time-compressed program designers are searching for teaching materials that can teach important concepts in multiple disciplines.

Second, consider the wide variety of ways in which an idea might be repeated:

- By the **teacher**, orally in class, in writing before or after class, or informally outside of class. For instance, the teacher can repeat ideas by repeating questions that help to surface similarities between the last class meeting and the current one.

- By the **students** in class, in learning teams, and out of class. For instance, the teacher can ask at the start of class whether the students would adhere to the same conclusion after a few days' reflection—and then revisit the issue near the end of the current class, after the discussion of the day's materials.

- By the **course materials and readings**, especially through the artful use of optional readings. Course design can build repetitive linkages from one day to the next through the use of materials that build upon each other.

- By a **visiting speaker**. For instance, a practicing professional can confirm the use and importance of a concept in daily practice, and extend students' grasp through examples that illustrate its application.

- By ad hoc **serendipitous materials** such as newspaper articles, graphs of related data, and cartoons. For instance, the alert instructor will see opportunities to relate current events to tools and concepts covered in the course. Soon, alert students will take the cue to bring in their own examples.

The mix of time frames and instruments affords an enormous variety of opportunities to repeat ideas. Here are five tactics that I have found to be especially useful for harnessing the power of repetition for student centered learning.

1. **At the start of each class** session, invite students to offer their "big ahas" or key learnings from the previous session. I write these on a side chalkboard, and quite often refer to them during that day's discussion. This emphasizes the connectivity of ideas from one case discussion to the next. Suppose the students don't identify the "ahas" that you have in mind, and instead offer inapt "ahas." I use these as occasions to argue back with challenging questions, redirect their thinking with contrary evidence, and suggest alternative ways of thinking about the subject.

2. **In every few classes**, offer some comments on the path of ideas, and how they are gathering together toward future learnings. I have done this both orally in a few minutes of class time, and in writing, in the form of module notes--these cover important ideas, questions, and issues, with the intent of giving students more to think about rather than relieving the students of the effort to figure things out for themselves.

3. Design your course like **a story that has a few dominant themes** to be repeated frequently and a number of subsidiary ideas to be built. Great stories have a beginning that creates tension or inquiry, a middle that enriches the problem, and an ending that revisits the tension and resolves it. For instance, in an introductory course on finance, the dominant themes might be capital market efficiency, prices modeled as the present values of future cash flows, value creation, risk, and return. I have case studies that raise these issues at an intuitive level—I use these cases to open the course. Then I structure the course as a series of modules, each of which dwells on one theme and explores theories and applications. At the end, I use comprehensive cases again to illustrate the interrelatedness of the tools, concepts, and themes and to build confidence among students in their own newly found capabilities.

4. Carefully choose **required readings** that send a consistent message with the ideas repeated elsewhere in the course.

5. **Create many small opportunities** to reinforce, revisit, and repeat ideas. These might be in the form of brown-bag lunches where the students pick the topics or simply arriving early/leaving slowly from class and using the extra time to converse about important ideas.

Repetition is an important element of learning—maybe not the first element, but much more important than the current emphases on speed and brevity suggest. Even in the midst of binding time constraints, look for opportunities to revisit, review, and restate. Through repetition, students return to where they started and "know the place for the first time."

Chapter 22
The Power of Student Teams

"It often happens that two schoolboys can solve difficulties in their work for one another better than the master can. When you took the problem to a master, as we all remember, he was very likely to explain what you understood already, to add a great deal of information which you didn't want, and say nothing at all about the thing that was puzzling you.... The fellow-pupil can help more than the master because he knows less."

-- *C.S. Lewis*[93]

Teachers can try too hard: they can focus on teaching rather than learning, on control rather than guidance, on the material rather than the student. Too much Teacher can crowd out other important avenues of learning. Finding the right mixture of Teacher Presence is one of the subtle challenges confronting the instructor and program designer. Here is where using peer-based teaching tactics can help immensely.

Peer-based teaching brings students together in teams to prepare for regular case discussions, to develop special presentations or reports, or to simulate a role in an action learning exercise. Study teams complement individual work and plenary case discussions. A number of professional schools form them at the program level at the beginning of the educational process. Many individual instructors form teams at the course level. Meeting rooms and other resources are made available for the teams. More importantly, time is created in the schedule for teams to do their work. The instructor typically offers some guidance for the teams such as study questions for a case, a detailed assignment for a report or presentation, or a briefing for an action learning exercise.

Though common to many degree and executive programs in business, student teams are relatively unused in professional curricula. I have relied significantly on team-based learning activities and have had an excellent experience with them in areas such as daily preparation for class discussion, simulations of merger negotiations, and team-based reports. Team-based learning carries a number of advantages:

1. **Better learning by the student.** This is because teams replicate the experience of discussion-based learning that occurs in the classroom. This kind of learning is

---

[93] C.S. Lewis. *Reflections on the Psalms* New York: Harvest Books, 1964.

better because it is self-paced, self-discovered, and self-appropriated. Quite simply, the student is challenged in ways that solo preparation cannot.

2. **Better use of the instructor's time.** Students who engage problems first in their study teams have a clearer sense of what they do not know. Their questions are sharper, thinking more critical, and sense of the larger flow of ideas is better because they challenge each other. This means that if a student visits an instructor with questions, the session is likely to offer more productive engagement.

3. **Better class discussions.** Students who participate in study teams usually arrive at class better prepared to discuss the case because they use this time to "warm up." They are more familiar with the facts of the situation, display a sense of the real problems, and typically have some completed analysis to share.

4. **Better preparation for professional life.** Many important problems in professional life today are handled in teams. Study teams simulate this kind of work and thereby help prepare students for life beyond school. A hot topic among leading organizations today is "knowledge transfer" among workers. By incorporating study teams into courses and programs, students learn skills of small-group teaching and study that prepares them for effective knowledge transfer.

5. **Better networking.** A subtle aim of most degree students and executive program participants is to build contacts with peers. It is a mistake to assume that the superficial greetings that occur over coffee and doughnuts are the basis for helpful networking. Really lasting personal networks emerge from earnest mutual effort. A Russian proverb says that to really know someone, you must eat a bag of salt together. In the context of learning in your subject, this depth of networking can be achieved through team-based preparation of case problems, reports, presentations, and simulations.

6. **Better program pacing.** Team meetings provide "breathers" for students in a fast-paced program. We see this most clearly in executive education programs. Because of the limited contact time with the executive participants, the temptation of teachers is to maximize the time in the classroom. This is usually a mistake. Mixing team time into the program can enhance participant satisfaction and learning.

7. **Better performance.** Teams usually out-perform individuals in activities such as preparing to discuss a case. Decision-makers benefit from multiple and fresh perspectives on problems that they can get from knowing how to work with teams.

If the use of teams is so good, why aren't they ubiquitous in university programs? Perhaps the individualistic nature of doctoral studies trains professors to think of learning as a solo experience. Also, there is the hubris of the instructor, the belief that what he or she has to say is vastly more important than anything the students could possibly say to one another. But the objections I have heard most often have been these:

- **It is costly.** Team activities take time, attention, and resources such as meeting rooms. Faculty feel stretched enough. Many schools simply don't have the space; to create teams would call attention to the resource constraint. Yet I have seen study teams thrive at commuter schools where there was no space to meet; the teams did their work at a nearby eatery or at student apartments. If teams can be used at a commuter school, the most difficult environment, there can be little excuse for not using them in other settings.

- **It is a free market;** let the students form teams if they want to. Why compel them to join? The reality is that you can never force successful team participation. But with sufficient motivation (e.g., through grading and exhortation), students usually choose to participate. The effort to form teams helps students who may find it difficult to join teams on their own: commuters; those whose first language is not English; single parents who have limited time flexibility; and introverts who make up a significant percentage of the population. Others need teams but may not know it, such as the self-appointed "expert" who would benefit from a reality check. Self-selected teams often form among likes, rather than opposites. But learning is probably greater within teams of opposites because they have a lower propensity toward lazy consensus and "groupthink." The heterogeneous needs and backgrounds of students argue for an active role by the instructor in designating teams.

- **The program does not have time for it.** When time runs short, the first activity to be cut is team study time, usually with unattractive results. For instance, instructors delivering a short executive education program needed to create time to accommodate an expert speaker in the program. Rather than cut into class time or a cocktail reception, they cut out a study team session. As a result, the affected case discussion was flat; and the students were tired by the time the speaker appeared. Neglecting group time can be costly.

- **Some students resist participating in teams,** claiming that it is a waste of time and that it interferes with their learning. If you hear this, you may have under-sold the importance of the study team. Often these students protest too much; ironically, they might benefit the most from participating in a team.

Introduce study teams, or any team-based activity from the outset of a course. Fold them into the basic design of the whole teaching effort. If team-based activities are new to the culture of your school, you should anticipate the need to explain and motivate repeatedly the importance of teams to student learning. In short executive programs, the whole faculty team must talk up the importance of the study teams. Here are a range of steps you can take to introduce the use of peer-based teaching in your course or program:

A. **Learn more about the use of teams in business today and what drives team success and failure.** A well-written starting point is the book, *The Wisdom of Teams*, by Jon R. Katzenbach and Douglas K. Smith (Harvard Business School Press, 1993). The book focuses on the use of teams in business rather than education, but it will help shape your thinking about the team-participation skills to develop among students today.

B. **Look for special team activities that might punctuate your course.** Review your course or program and think about carving out some task, project, or analysis that might provide a focal point for team activity, and/or a product to be generated by the team such as a presentation, report, or negotiation. Carefully devise written instructions to the team.

C. **Look for ways in which study groups might supplement or prepare for the regular class discussions.** If your course is a mixture of cases and lectures, you might anticipate and structure ways in which study groups would prepare for those classes.

D. **Organize teams and provide for their time and activity.** Choose members of the team on the basis of seeking maximum diversity within the team by age, gender, skills, race, nationality, work experience, etc.

E. **Motivate the teams.** Explain that the team assignment is not merely a matter of student convenience but is an important part of the learning experience. The way to get greatest gain from the course is by participating actively in a team. Research suggests that commitment is the primary driver of team success. Some motivational words by the instructor can help build this commitment.

F. **Offer team-based grading.** In my course, students evaluate each other on their contributions to two team-based activities (negotiation exercises and a report). The evaluation contributes to the class contribution grade, which accounts for 40-50 percent of the individual's final grade.

G. **Give team-based feedback.** When teams give a presentation to a class, invite visiting practitioners or other students to offer questions and suggestions, and even to grade it. When teams submit a paper, return comments to the team.

H. **Shape expectations about student performance.** Good students may be reluctant to represent as their own ideas the work that was actually generated in a group. Instructors should invite open acknowledgement: "This is my team's analysis—I'm not sure we sorted it all out, but here is where we are..."

I. **Encourage virtuality.** Videoconferencing by phone and Internet is available now and will improve by magnitudes as bandwidth increases. Students can easily swap text and spreadsheet files by email. Face-to-face exchange is crucial for building trust and familiarity, but once these are in place, teams should be encouraged to function from any distance.

J. **Offer team-building activities.** Program leaders can arrange events for teams to build trust and familiarity rapidly. Ropes courses are now a common feature in many university programs. A second resource is the team mentor: a senior student who has had a good experience in a study team and can coach novices toward building their own effective teams. Leaders and team mentors need to discuss strategies for good team experiences. For instance, many students use team meeting time simply to get familiar with the discussion materials. Instead, students should fully prepare the materials in advance of team meetings, and then use the group time to test their analysis and views with the group. Group meetings should be organized, focused, and short, not protracted and open-ended.

In conclusion, the use of student teams embodies three bits of wisdom. First, one learns greatly from one's peers. Second, two to eight heads (and hearts and pairs of hands) are better than one. Teams bring out the richness of cases, problems, and analysis. And third, learning by doing beats learning by watching. What one does in teams is strengthen one's abilities to manage interpersonal processes. In most professional work, interpersonal processes are a daily fact of life. The power of student teams is easily obscured and forgotten. Yet it can give an immense boost to your teaching efforts, and ultimately, student learning.

Chapter 23
Opening a Course[94]

"Well begun is half done."
-- English proverb

Professor C. Roland Christensen once remarked that the management of *beginnings* and *endings* was among the most important, but least appreciated, professional skills. Professors are trained to focus on the substantive middle, the "beef," in the intellectual burger. All too often the buns must fend for themselves. Such neglect can be costly. A faulty start to a course can create a legacy that will haunt you for the rest of the course, or worse. "A bad beginning makes a bad ending," said Euripides. The reality is that first impressions are hugely important within the classroom because of the expectations they can create about the remainder of the course. How can one get a course launched well?

Let's begin with what the instructor should try to do at the opening. Note that many of us regard the opening of a course to run from the first session to whenever the course hits its stride. That can occur on day one of the course, or after day ten. You'll know that you have concluded the opening when students begin to teach each other and the class assumes the quality of a community. The comments that follow focus mainly on the first day, though they easily extend onward in time. The opening of a course carries these primary aims:

1. **Communicate a vision about substance, a value proposition.** On the first day students seek a sense of what the course is about. "Without a vision, the people are lost," says the Proverb. This vision is communicated in many ways including the title of the course, the syllabus, selection of readings, etc. Student word-of-mouth conveys a vision as well, which is not always flawless. The opening of the course should help to align student vision—this kind of alignment can forestall misunderstandings later. This vision forms the basis for a value proposition to the students: "If you take this course, do the work, contribute actively to discussions, etc., here's what you can expect to learn...."

---

[94] This chapter draws upon a roundtable discussion I organized with Paul Irvine, Andrew Karolyi, John Pringle, Ahmad Rahnema, William Sihler, Nikhil Varaiya, and Mark Zenner. To these friends I give my thanks for a stimulating exchange. The original record of this discussion was reported in *FEN Educator*, and can be downloaded without charge from http://papers.ssrn.com/sol3/papers.cfm?abstract_id=178748.

2. **Frame expectations about the contract.** The classroom "contract" consists of mutual expectations about class preparation, attendance, class participation, and norms of discussion and conduct. Cold-calling and what constitutes an acceptable discussion opening must be established. It is also useful to convey to students that not every class will reach a definitive closing and that you may choose to let students ruminate. Ultimately, the classroom contract is a basis for trust. Donald Hambrick notes that "the core ingredient in trust is reliability." He gives new classes a commitment to:

   - "put together a well-conceived, contemporary course…

   - be fully prepared for each class…

   - listen attentively…

   - respect your point of view, but also to register, at the time or possibly later, my own point of view…

   - evaluate your written work promptly and constructively."[95]

3. **Establish leadership and credibility.** The successful entry of a leader into a new situation establishes a kind of command over followers based on respect for the leader's skills and trust in his or her purposes. Good entry establishes the leader as a credible guide through a problem or opportunity. It is crucially important for the instructor to take actions at the opening that create respect and trust.

4. **Build energy and motivation.** From the start, the instructor needs to be an enthusiast for the subject, and to convey it with energy and sparkle. Many students come to your subject curious and perhaps apprehensive about this quantitative subject. Enthusiasm helps less confident students to meet your subject and more confident students to excel.

5. **The opening should contribute solidly to the students' mastery of the subject.** I reject the idea that the first day should be written off as administrative overhead. The content of the opening sends signals about the rest of the course. I find that good students simply want to get on with their learning--they look for a return on their investment even in the first day. Try to give it to them.

How are these aims to be achieved? Most students don't like to hear lectures about vision, contract, and enthusiasm. Realistically, the opening class is a blur to most students anyway. Instead the instructor needs to walk the talk, set an example in the first class

---

[95] Donald C. Hambrick, "Teaching as Leading," in *Researchers Hooked on Teaching*, Rae Andre and Peter J. Frost, eds., Thousand Oaks, CA: Sage Publications, 1997 page 250.

about the rest of the course. This approach implies a number of action items for the instructor at the opening:

a. **Choose cases or teaching materials for the opening that set sound themes** for the course and perhaps leave time for commentary that you may need to offer about the course. Also, these should be materials in which you are confident: they should work well with this type of audience; you should have mastered the teaching challenge in the materials; it should be a case problem that you like.

b. **Study the audience**, and get to know them in advance. As argued in Chapter 9, knowledge of the students helps develop good rapport. If your school provides any biographical information on the students, study it. Look for opportunities to call on students in the first class based on their prior experience.

c. **Scout out the classroom** well in advance of the class. Figure out how to run the systems. Order materials you may need. If the desks or tables are arranged in the wrong way, ask that they be rearranged in a horseshoe pattern.

d. **Polish and arrange the supporting materials** such as electronic resources (e.g., Excel files), website, and syllabus. These ancillary materials are an important avenue on which students encounter the course at the opening. Flaws, miscommunication, and general disorganization can undercut a strong effort in the classroom.

e. When you meet the students, **get on to the business of the course quickly**—teaching and learning. Avoid lengthy icebreakers or boring discussion of administrative issues.

f. Remember that the overarching aim of the course opening is to **strike an effective "contract"** with students that promotes their ability to teach themselves and that helps to elevate the group into a learning community.

If you feel a need to make any concluding remarks on the first day, focus on how this opening discussion raises many questions and themes to be addressed by the course. Set the themes and sell the themes, saying why they are important. Be extremely careful about using handouts, closing lecture, or case analysis "hints" in the first session, lest students come to expect them as a routine. Plainly, however, the opening stage of a course deserves careful reflection on the goals of the opening, but also the means by which those goals are to be achieved.

Chapter 24
Shaping the Classroom Contract:
How the Teacher Might Brief the Student
About Preparing for a Case Method Class

In opening the discussion method course, the instructor tries to shape a contract and build a community. This chapter extends the discussion in Chapter 23 by illustrating the possible form and content of this shaping and building effort, including:

- **Writing.** It is important for the students to have in writing an expression of your expectations for their participation in the course. Many instructors recoil from this, in the belief that it invites dispute over the details. My experience suggests the opposite: written expectations express a clear vision to which you can return if necessary throughout the course. Even though you are laying down the law, try to do this in a coaching fashion. An example of this appears in the Appendix of this chapter. It is a note to the student published in the front of my book of case studies in finance where I use it to help set expectations about the case learning experience. You could distribute a briefing such as this to your students, and support it with similar sentiments in the course syllabus.

- **Oral comments.** At the start of a course, students tend not to read contract-setting documents with extreme care. Take a little time to convey the gist of these ideas, and to remind the students to read the documents. I would be reluctant to cannibalize much discussion with a briefing, and therefore prefer to leave the details to a written note.

- **Actions, in and outside of class.** It is important to behave in ways consistent with the contract and community that you seek to build. One's actions really do speak louder than words. Such actions might include:
    - **Encouraging the formation of study groups.** This might be part of your oral briefing at the start of the course, but you could also support the expectation about groups by giving group-based assignments and repeatedly asking students, "What did your study team conclude?" "Where did your study team encounter difficulty?" And "Did your study team agree with your personal views?"
    - **Cold-calling students** to open the class discussion on the expectation that they come prepared to discuss the material. A cold call is usually the

opening question of the day that asks the student to begin the discussion with his or her analysis of the material.

- o **Requesting a "stand."** Part of the contract should be that preparation is not complete until the student has formed a view or actionable recommendation about the material. Early in a course, students may not come to class prepared to take a stand—here is where the instructor, in coaching fashion, can help a student develop a stand in class: this sends a strong signal about completeness of preparation to other students.

- o **Emphasizing respect for diversity of opinion, and of the discussion process.** The success of the discussion method depends vitally on the surfacing of new ideas. Over the course of many years the teacher will hear error, falsehood, or worse—to hear them is not to endorse them, but rather to enable discussion to correct them. Discussion leadership must set a tone of basic respect for divergent opinions. Tone-setting occurs through actions such as pausing after asking a question so that tentative students have a moment to frame their thoughts before speaking, discouraging interruptions while a student speaks, through questions helping an inarticulate student express an idea, and inviting alternative points of view.

- • **Comments to students outside of class.** Through informal conversations the instructor can shape the classroom contract. Compliments on good discussion are always welcome by students, and serve to reinforce their future contributions. One can steer students away from less helpful contributions with coaching comments such as "Next time you offer your ideas, think about ..."

Is all this really necessary? If the discussion method is about student self-discovery, shouldn't the instructor simply get on with teaching, and not worry about this kind of stage-setting? The cost of a flawed course launch can be very high for the instructor (and students). Investing in this kind of shaping activity both hedges against unfortunate outcomes, and promotes student learning. The student-centered teacher doesn't have much choice in the matter: actively shaping the contract and building the community is fundamental to the success of the discussion method.

Appendix to Chapter 24
A Note to the Student:
How to Prepare and Discuss Cases[96]

"Get a good idea and stay with it. Dog it and work at it until it's done and done right."
-- Walt Disney

You enroll in a "case method" course, pick up the book of case studies or the stack of loose-leaf cases, and get ready for the first class meeting. If this is your first experience with case discussions, the odds are that you are a little anxious about how to prepare for this course. That's fairly normal but something you should try to break through quickly in order to gain the maximum from your studies. Quick breakthroughs come from a combination of good attitude, good "infrastructure," and good execution—this note offers some tips.

Good Attitude

Students learn best that which they teach themselves. Passive and mindless learning is ephemeral. Active, mindful, learning simply sticks. The case method makes learning sticky by placing you in situations that require invention of tools and concepts *in your own terms*. The most successful case students share a set of characteristics that drive self-teaching:

1. **Personal initiative, self-reliance.** Case studies rarely suggest how to proceed. Professors are more like guides on a long hike: they can't carry you, but they can show you the way. You must arrive at the destination under your own power. You must figure out the case on your own. To teach yourself means that you must sort ideas out in ways that make sense to you, personally. To teach yourself is to give yourself two gifts: the idea you are trying to learn, and greater self-confidence in your own ability to master the world.

---

[96] Published in R.F. Bruner, *Case Studies in Finance: Managing for Corporate Value* Creation Burr Ridge: McGraw-Hill/Irwin, 4th ed. 2002. Loose-leaf copies of this note may be ordered for classroom use from the Darden Case Collection, (Mailto:dardencases@virginia.edu), catalogue number UVA-G-0561.

2. **Curiosity, a zest for exploration as an end in itself.** Richard P. Feynman, who won the Nobel Prize in Physics in 1965, was once asked whether his key discovery was worth it. He replied, "...[the Nobel Prize is] a pain in the...I don't like honors...The prize is the pleasure of finding the thing out, the kick in the discovery, the observation that other people use it [my work]—those are the real things, the honors are unreal to me."[97]

3. **A willingness to take risks.** Risk-taking is at the heart of all learning. Usually one learns more from failures than successes.

4. **Patience and persistence.** Case studies are messy, a realistic reflection of the fact that managers don't manage problems, they manage messes. Initially, reaching a solution will seem to be the major challenge. But once you reach *a* solution, you may discover other possible solutions, and face the choice among the best alternatives.

5. **An orientation to community and discussion.** Much of the power of the case method derives from a willingness to *talk* with others about your ideas and/or your points of confusion. This is one of the paradoxes of the case method: you must teach yourself, but not in a vacuum. The poet T.S. Eliot said, "There is no life not lived in community." Talking seems like such an inefficient method of sorting through the case; but, if exploration is an end in itself, then talking is the only way. Furthermore, talking is an excellent means of testing your own mastery of ideas, of rooting out points of confusion, and of preparing you for professional life.

6. **Trust in the process.** The learnings from a case-method course are impressive. They arrive cumulatively over time. In many cases, the learnings continue well after the course has finished. Occasionally, these learnings hit you with the force of a tsunami. But generally, the learnings creep in quietly but powerfully, like the tide. After the case course, you will look back and see that your thinking, mastery, and appreciation for finance have changed dramatically. The key point is that you should not measure the success of your progress on the basis of any single case discussion. Trust that in the cumulative work over many cases you will gain the mastery you seek.

---

[97] Richard P. Feynman, *The Pleasure of Finding Things Out*, Cambridge, Perseus Publishing, 1999, page 12.

Good Infrastructure

"Infrastructure" consists of all the resources that the case student can call upon. Some of this is simply given to you by the professor: case studies, assignment questions, supporting references to textbooks or articles, and computer data or models. But you can go much farther to help yourself. Consider these steps:

1. **Find a quiet place to study. Spend at least 90 minutes there for each case study.** Each case has subtleties to it, which you will miss unless you can concentrate. After two or three visits, your quiet place will take on the attributes of a habit: you will slip into a working attitude more easily. Be sure to spend enough time in the quiet place to give yourself a chance to really engage the case.

2. **Get a business dictionary.** If you are new to business and finance, some of the terms will seem foreign; if English is not your first language, *many* of the terms will seem foreign if not bizarre. Get into the habit of looking up terms that you don't know. The benefit of this becomes cumulative.

3. **Skim a business newspaper each day; read a business magazine.** Reading a newspaper or magazine helps build a *context* for the case study you are trying to solve at the moment, and helps you make connections between the case study and current events. The terminology of business and finance that you see in the publications helps reinforce your use of the dictionary and hastens your mastery of terms you will see in the cases. Your learning by reading business periodicals is cumulative.

4. **Learn the basics of spreadsheet modeling on a computer.** Many case studies now have supporting data available for analysis in spreadsheet files, such as Microsoft Excel. Analyzing the data on a computer rather than by hand both speeds up your work and extends your reach.

5. **Form a study group.** The ideas in many cases are deep; the analysis can get complex. *You will learn more, and perform better in class participation, by discussing the cases together in a learning team.* Your team should devote an average of an hour to each case. High performance teams show a number of common attributes:

   a. Members commit to the success of the team.

   b. The team plans ahead, leaving time for contingencies.

   c. The team meets regularly.

141

d. Team members show up for meetings and are *prepared* to contribute.

e. There may or may not be a formal leader, but assignments are clear. Team members meet their assigned obligations.

6. **Get to know your professor.** In the case method, students inevitably learn more from one another than from the instructor. But the teacher is part of the learning infrastructure too: a resource to be used wisely. Never troll for answers in advance of a case discussion. Do your homework; use classmates and learning teams to clear up most questions so you can focus on the meatiest issues with the teacher. Be very organized and focused about what you would like to discuss. Remember that teachers like to learn too: if you reveal a new insight about a case or bring a clipping about a related issue in current events, the professor and student both gain from their time together. Ultimately, the best payoff to the professor is the "aha" in the student's eyes when he or she masters the idea.

Good Execution

Good attitude and infrastructure must be employed properly—one needs good execution. The extent to which a student learns depends on how the case study is approached. What can one do to gain the maximum from the study of these cases?

1. **Reading the case**. The very first time you read any case, look for the forest not the trees. This requires that your first reading be quick. Do not begin taking notes on the first round; instead, read the case like a magazine article. The first few paragraphs of a well-constructed case usually say something about the problem—read those carefully. Then quickly read the rest of the case, seeking mainly a sense of the scope of the problems, and what information the case contains to help resolve them. Leaf through the exhibits, looking for what information they hold, rather than for any analytical insights. At the conclusion of the first pass, read any supporting articles or notes that your instructor may have recommended.

2. **Getting into the case situation. Develop your "awareness."** With the broader perspective in mind, the second and more detailed reading will be more productive. The reason is that as you now encounter details, your mind will be able to organize them in some useful fashion rather than inventorying them randomly. Making linkages among case details is necessary toward solving the case. At this point you can take the notes that will set up your analysis.

The most successful students project themselves into the position of the decision-maker because this perspective helps them link case details as well as develop a stand on the case problem. Assignment questions may help you do this; but it is a good idea to get into the habit of doing it yourself. Here are the kinds of questions you might try to answer in preparing every case:

A. Who are the protagonists in the case? Who must take action on the problem? What do they have at stake? What pressures are they under?

B. In what business is the company? What is the nature of its product? What is the nature of demand for that product? What is the firm's distinctive competence? With whom does it compete?[98] What is the structure of the industry? Is the firm comparatively strong or weak? In what ways?

C. What are the goals of the firm? What is the firm's strategy in pursuit of these goals? (The goals and strategy might be explicitly stated, or they may be implicit in the way the firm does business.) What are the firm's apparent functional policies in marketing (e.g., push- versus-pull strategy), production (e.g., in labor relations, use of new technology, distributed production vs. centralized), and finance (e.g., the use of debt financing, payment of dividends)? Financial and business strategies can be inferred from analysis of financial ratios and a sources and uses of funds statement.

D. How well has the firm performed in pursuit of its goals? (The answer to this question calls for simple analysis using financial ratios, such as the DuPont system, compound growth rates, and measures of value creation.)

The larger point of this phase of your case preparation is to broaden your awareness of issues. Perhaps the most successful investor in history, Warren Buffett, said, "Any player unaware of the fool in the market probably is the fool in the market." Awareness is an important attribute of successful managers.

3. **Defining the problem.** A common trap for many executives is to assume that the issue at hand is the real problem most worthy of their time rather than a symptom

---

[98]Think broadly about competitors. Mark Twain wrote in *A Connecticut Yankee in King Arthur's Court*, "The best swordsman in the world doesn't need to fear the second best swordsman in the world; no, the person for him to be afraid of is some ignorant antagonist who has never had a sword in his hand before; he doesn't do the thing he ought to do, and so the expert isn't prepared for him; he does the thing he ought not to do; and it often catches the expert out and ends him on the spot." (Reissue edition [June 1994], Bantam Classic and Loveswept; ISBN: 0553211439.)

of some larger problem that *really* deserves their time. For instance, a lender is often asked to advance funds to help tide a firm over a cash shortfall. Careful study may reveal that the key problem is not a cash shortfall, but rather it is product obsolescence, unexpected competition, or careless cost management. Even in cases where the decision is fairly narrowly defined (such as in a capital expenditure choice), the "problem" generally turns out to be the believability of certain key assumptions. Students who are new to the case method tend to focus narrowly in defining problems and often overlook the influence that the larger setting has on the problem. In doing this, the student develops narrow specialist habits, never achieving the general manager perspective. It is useful and important for you to define the problem yourself and, in the process, validate the problem as suggested by the protagonist in the case.

4. **Analysis: run the numbers and go to the heart of the matter.** Virtually all finance cases require numerical analysis. This is good because figure-work lends rigor and structure to your thinking. But some cases, reflecting reality, invite you to explore blind alleys. If you are new to finance, even these explorations will help you learn.[99] The best case students develop an instinct for where to devote their analysis. Economy of effort is desirable. If you have invested wisely in problem definition, economical analysis tends to follow. For instance, a student might assume that a particular case is meant to exercise financial forecasting skills and will spend two or more hours preparing a detailed forecast, instead of preparing a simpler forecast in one hour and conducting a sensitivity analysis based on key assumptions in the next hour. An executive rarely thinks of a situation as having to do with a forecasting method or discounting or any other technique, but rather thinks of it as a problem of judgment, deciding on which people or concepts or environmental conditions to bet. The best case analyses get down to the *key bets* on which the executive is wagering the prosperity of the firm, and his or her career. Get to the business issues quickly and avoid lengthy churning through relatively unimportant calculations.

5. **Prepare to participate: take a stand.** To develop analytical insights without making recommendations is useless to executives, and drains the case study experience of some of its learning power. A stand means having a point of view about the problem, a recommendation, and an analysis to back up both of them. The lessons most worth learning all come from taking a stand. From that truth

---

[99]Case analysis is often iterative: an understanding of the big issues invites an analysis of details—then the details may restructure the big issues and invite the analysis of other details. In some cases, getting to the "heart of the matter" will mean just such iteration.

flows the educative force of the case method. In the typical case, the student is projected into the position of an executive who must do something in response to a problem. It is this choice of what to do that constitutes the executive's "stand." Over the course of a career, an executive who takes stands gains wisdom. If the stand provides an effective resolution of the problem, so much the better for all concerned. If it does not, however, the wise executive analyzes the reasons for the failure and may learn even more than from a success. As Theodore Roosevelt wrote:

The credit belongs to the man[100] who is actually in the arena—whose face is marred by dust and sweat and blood...who knows the great enthusiasms, the great devotions—and spends himself in a worthy cause—who at best if he wins knows the thrills of high achievement—and if he fails, at least fails while daring greatly so that his place shall never be with those cold and timid souls who know neither victory nor defeat.

6. **In class: participate actively in support of your conclusions, but be open to new insights.** Of course, one can have a stand without the world being any wiser. To take a stand in case discussions means to participate actively in the discussion and to advocate your stand until new facts or analysis emerge to warrant a change.[101] Learning by the case method is not a spectator sport. A classic error many students make is to bring into the case method classroom the habits of the lecture hall (i.e., passively absorbing what other people say). These habits fail miserably in the case method classroom because they guarantee that one only absorbs the truths and fallacies uttered by others. The purpose of case study is to develop and exercise *one's own* skills and judgment. This takes practice and participation—just as in a sport. Here are two good general suggestions: (1) defer significant note taking until after class and (2) strive to contribute to every case discussion.

7. **Immediately after class: jot down notes, corrections, and questions.** Don't overinvest in taking notes during class—that just cannibalizes "air time" in which you could be learning through discussing the case. But immediately after, collect

---

[100]Today, a statement such as this would surely recognize women as well.

[101]There is a difference between taking a stand and pigheadedness. Nothing is served by clinging to your stand to the bitter end in the face of better analysis or common sense. Good managers recognize new facts and arguments as they come to light—and adapt.

your learnings and questions in notes that will capture your thinking. Of course, ask a fellow student or your teacher questions that will help clarify issues that still puzzle you.

8. **Once a week, flip through notes. Make a list of your questions and pursue answers.** Take an hour each weekend to review your notes from class discussions during the past week. This will help build your grasp of the flow of the course. Studying a subject by the case method is like building a large picture with small mosaic tiles. It helps to step back to see the big picture. But the main objective should be to make an inventory of anything you are unclear about: terms, concepts, and calculations. Work your way through this inventory with classmates, learning teams, and ultimately the instructor. This kind of review and follow-up builds your self-confidence and prepares you to participate more effectively in future case discussions.

Conclusion: Focus on Process, and Results Will Follow

View the case method experience as a series of opportunities to test your mastery of techniques and your business judgment. If you seek a list of axioms to be etched in stone, you are bound to disappoint yourself. As in real life, there are virtually no "right" answers to a case in the sense that a scientific or engineering problem has an exact solution—though there may be many wrong answers. Jeff Milman has said, "The answers worth getting are never found in the back of the book." What matters is that you obtain a way of thinking about business situations that you can carry from one job (or career) to the next. In the case method it is largely true that *how you learn is what you learn.*

Chapter 25
Helping Discussions to "Catch Fire"

In a great discussion-based class, students experience a convergence of energy and thought. An idea or comment nags several students, won't let go, and spreads. The discussion assumes a life of its own, almost apart from any direction you might offer. Students exercise leadership for expressing and testing ideas; they replicate the exploratory process in class. In an intangible instant, one perspective seems to sweep the class; the light goes on; the class "clicks." This is one of the most gratifying moments in teaching, and is something that many teachers consciously strive for. Would that it happened every time—but it does not. Some class discussions run flat, despite one's best efforts. Others spin out of control or dive into an abyss of false thinking. Both the good and the bad instances reveal the surprising spread of an idea, attitude, or energy. What can the instructor do to encourage the good outcomes, and thwart the bad?

The viral spread of ideas

Malcolm Gladwell's book, *The Tipping Point*[102], offers some insights relevant to discussion leadership. Gladwell writes, "The tipping point . . . is the best way to understand the emergence of fashion trends . . . or the phenomena of word of mouth or any number of the other mysterious changes that mark everyday life . . . think of them as epidemics. Ideas and products and messages and behaviors spread just like viruses do."[103] A tipping point is that moment when an epidemic begins to grow explosively. Epidemiologists attribute tipping points to three main factors. First is the stickiness of the virus. Second is the favorable context of the infection. And third is the presence of key people who transmit the spread. The point where class discussion "clicks" is a tipping point: an idea catches hold and spreads quickly. Teachers seeking to motivate a tipping point in classroom discussion might consider the three requisites of the viral spread of ideas:

1. **Sticky messages.** These are compelling notions that are memorable. Such messages must have substance, something worth remembering. This implies that we should adopt cases or teaching materials that challenge thinking, rather

---

[102] Malcolm Gladwell, *The Tipping Point: How Little Things Can Make a Big Difference*, Boston: Little Brown & Company, copyright 2000, ISBN 0-316-31696-2.
[103] *Ibid.*, page 7.

than merely describe, and that contain big ideas. Sticky messages also have a memorable form. Often the teacher will struggle over how to make the message more contagious when the issue really is how to get it to stick, to make it memorable. At any point in time, numerous courses clamor for students' attention, not to mention their career ambitions, social lives, and frustrations of daily living. Sticky messages penetrate the fog created by these distractions. Is the idea reinforced in multiple ways (text reading, comments by the instructor, a problem set, a case discussion, a video)? Does the instructor deliver the message with humor, drama, or some other attention-getting device? Is the message conveyed with clarity?

2. **Favorable conditions.** Contagion spreads more easily in some circumstances than others. One needs to create a course culture and classroom in which students can truly focus on the exchange of ideas and in which that exchange is fostered, indeed required. Many school classrooms seat the students facing the lecturer—consider changing the seating to favor face-to-face contact among students. The dominant model at many schools is *passive learning.* Instead, consider sharply defining the model in your course as *active learning*—the course opening, syllabus, notes to students, etc., are all devices for creating conditions favorable to the viral spread of ideas.

3. **Involvement by key players.** The teacher is important, but the really key carriers of ideas in classroom discussions are students who are thought leaders of the class (those who step on the accelerator) and/or other students (perhaps those at the trailing end of the performance distribution) who brake the forward movement of the class. Effective teachers display a heightened awareness to these key students in the class. A tipping point is enhanced where a teacher's resources (e.g., teacher's attention, demands, time) are used to enlist these key carriers for the benefit of the class. Gladwell offers a taxonomy of three kinds of key players to look out for: connectors, mavens, and salesmen.

   a. **Connectors** simply know lots of people and, especially, the right kinds of people. They have a gift for making connections and telling others the news. The existence of a network of acquaintance is crucial to tipping. Student leaders probably fit in this category.

   b. **Mavens** are people who not only accumulate knowledge, but who also want to teach it to others. They are motivated not only by their mastery of a topic but also by a simple desire to help, perhaps as a way of getting attention. Students who have worked in the subject field of your course may be able to speak with enough authority to attain the deference of others.

c. **Salesmen** persuade the audience when it is unmoved by the connector (who tells) and the maven (who teaches). Gladwell cites studies that emphasize the role of nonverbal behavior in the success of the salesmen such as smiling and head nodding. Most classes of students contain a measurable fraction skilled at persuasion.

One can imagine other categories as well. But these three are sufficient to stimulate the teacher's thinking. The rather large implication of this for teachers is that it may pay to find and attend to key players in one's class.

Follow the energy

If you want to stimulate active classroom discussion, the first rule is *follow the energy of the students.* This may take you off course from your teaching plan, and will require careful listening and acute judgment about how much wandering to allow. But in my experience, the apparent meanderings of students who are reasonably well motivated and prepared often lead to important learning. As the saying goes, not all who wander are lost. My bias would be to follow the energy for a bit, see where it leads, and judge whether the destination is worthy. The decision to do so is challenging, as a colleague's note to me illustrates:

> In class today, several controversial comments about dividend investor clienteles fanned the flames of class discussion. The students were literally climbing out of their seats to get into the fray. But, rather than let the class discussion really "catch fire," I elected to douse the discussion because my teaching plan called for spending more time on the issues of debt capacity. As soon as I turned the discussion, all of the energy in the class instantly evaporated. I knew I had made a mistake. Striking the right balance and knowing when to let the fire go with the wind is very tricky.

Conclusion

Ideas can spread virally. The quality of the idea, favorable conditions, and the intervention of key players influence the rate of spread. Of these three elements, the importance of attending to key players is a surprise for the novice instructor. One can absorb guidance on the first two elements (message and context) fairly quickly. But simply seeing the role of thought leaders in the classroom and drawing on them effectively is a difficult skill to learn. Students themselves may not want to be used to further the teacher's agenda; the teacher must find a way to enlist their help—asking the deep, general, key questions is essential to this process.

Getting classroom discussion to "catch fire" is a multidimensional challenge that must be managed actively. Three elements (sticky ideas, context, and key players) offer a framework for diagnosing the success of one's classroom efforts and for strategizing about future discussions.

Chapter 26
How Tough to Be; How to Be Tough

"He knows not his own strength that hath not met adversity."
-- Ben Jonson

So, boy, don't you turn back.
Don't you set down on the steps
'Cause you finds it kiner hard.
Don't you fall now—
For I'se still goin', honey
I's still climbin';
And life for me ain't been no crystal stair.
--Langston Hughes, *Mother to Son*

A man invited Nasrudin to go hunting with him, but mounted him on a horse which was too slow. The Mulla said nothing. Soon the hunt outpaced him and was out of sight. It began to rain heavily, and there was no shelter. All the members of the hunt got soaked through. Nasrudin, however, as soon as the rain started, took off all his clothes and folded them. Then he sat down on the pile. As soon as the rain stopped, he dressed himself and went back to his host's house for lunch. Nobody could work out why he was dry. With all the speed of their horses they had not been able to reach shelter on that plain.

"It was the horse you gave me," said Nasrudin.

The next day he was given a fast horse and his host took the slow one. Rain fell again. The horse was so slow that the host got wetter than ever, riding at a snail's pace to his house. Nasrudin carried out the same procedure as before. When he got back to the house he was dry.

"It is your fault!" shouted his host. "You made me ride this terrible horse."

"Perhaps," said Nasrudin, "you did not contribute anything of your own to the problem of keeping dry?"

--Idries Shah, "Dry in the Rain," from
The Pleasantries of the Incredible Mulla Nasrudin

"Fear is an instructor of great sagacity, and the herald of all revolutions."
-- Ralph Waldo Emerson

The tough teacher is a familiar heavy in film and literature: martinet, boor, hellion, or iceman. Such characterizations are a repugnant self-image to most teachers. Perhaps for this reason the tough teacher seems to be a fading breed on campuses. It is hard to imagine one who is tough *and* compassionate, student-centered, learning-focused and successful as measured by conventional student ratings. But the quotations of Emerson, Jonson, Hughes, and Shah can feed our imagination in useful ways. Their lessons are important because how tough one should be is almost the hardest choice about teaching style that an instructor must make. Erring by too much or too little suboptimizes student learning. Then, too, one must choose *how* to be tough. The limitless combinations of content (how tough to be) and form (how to be tough) enrich the dilemma. Where can the instructor—particularly the novice—find guidance? One could listen to the students, especially their teaching evaluations. But student feedback is an imperfect guide for calibrating one's style[104]. A second approach would be to follow the examples of one's colleagues. But, as the phenomenon of grade inflation suggests, following the crowd sometimes results in a race to the bottom. Third, one could imitate an exemplar with whom one studied in the past. But exemplars became that way because of how they responded to *their* circumstances; what you need is a response to *your* situation. This chapter argues that a concern for learning outcomes is the best lamp with which to find one's way through these dilemmas. It helps immensely to have a *view* about toughness in teaching: why and how to be tough.

Three dimensions of tough

What it means to be a tough instructor is best described from the student's point of view. Several books offer this view for graduate studies in law (Turow (1997)), medicine (Konner (1987)), engineering (White (1991)), and business (Cohen (1973), Ewing (1990)), Reid (1994)), and Robinson (1994)). In all of these books, the tough instructor and/or the toughness of the program are dominant themes. These accounts suggest that toughness is apparent in at least three dimensions: grading, workload or assignments, and classroom teaching.

Grading

White's (1991) account of graduate education in engineering at MIT is dominated by a fear of flunking out. Robinson (1994) writes about Stanford's MBA program,

> "At any business school the first year is the year of drama. It is the year of new faces and new surroundings. It is also the year of loneliness, self-doubt, and constant, unyielding pressure. For a great many students there come moments during the first year when, often for the first time in their lives, they wonder, quite seriously, whether they will fail."[105]

---

[104] For more on interpreting student evaluations, see Chapter 15, "Taking Stock: Evaluations from Students."
[105] Robinson (1994) page 5.

Grading stimulates a fear of failure. Tough graders amplify that fear. Students view an instructor to be a "tough" grader when he or she gives A's to the top small percentage of students, and C's or F's to the bottom small percentage. The too-tough instructor grades punitively: "the course didn't go the way I wanted, so I flunked 'em." The too-easy instructor doles out A's and rarely awards C's, a more common phenomenon these days. Grade inflation within colleges and universities is drawing renewed attention. In arguing against Harvard's granting academic honors to 91 percent of its student body in 2001, Professor Harvey Mansfield[106] argued that grade inflation reflects the declining authority of instructors. He wrote:

> "A professor, I conceive, should be part midwife, part taskmaster. The midwife—Socrates' famous metaphor—draws out the good that is already there. But since it is not enough merely to express oneself, the taskmaster sets the student to work. And for this a professor needs authority…When I refer to the lost authority of professors, there is more at stake than their self-importance. What matters is the atmosphere in which students are educated: Will it be demanding or forgiving?"

The debates over grade inflation at many universities today stimulate reflection on toughness in grading, as well as in assignments and classroom leadership.

Assignments

The higher one goes on the educational ladder, the higher are expectations for effort and mastery. Graduate school *is* tough in terms of workloads: the intellectual problems are more difficult and there are lots of them. Konner describes the life of medical residents:

> "The residents are under the greatest pressure they ever have been or will ever be under. They are outrageously overworked, sleep-deprived, overburdened with responsibility, bewildered by a barrage of ever-changing facts, and oppressed by the medical hierarchy, of which they are on the lowest rung….The president of the American Association of Medical Colleges referred to the process as 'brutal.'"[107]

---

[106] See especially Mansfield's "To B or not to B" in *Wall Street Journal*, December 20, 2001 page A16. A related article by him is, "Grade Inflation: It's Time to Face the Facts," *Chronicle of Higher Education*, April 6, 2001, http://chronicle.com/review, page B4.

[107] Konner (1987) pages 363 and 369.

Cohen quoted two first-year MBA students at Harvard:

> "It's a tense situation, but my attitude is that I'm going to do it. And, of course, you know, after the fact we will probably see that it was really not quite that bad by any means. But, nevertheless, when you're going through it, it...it seems terrible. It seems *terrible*. And I go to, you know, go to bed at night, at two o'clock in the morning and look up at the ceiling and say, you know: "What am I doing here? What am I doing at this place?"...Initially I felt I couldn't cope with the Harvard Business School...this is pretty rough here...But I just felt so far behind in terms of what I knew about what went on in business and about the effect, the immense effect that business has on everybody's life. It really shocked me....it was different from anything I'd ever experienced."[108]

Perhaps the workload perceptions in graduate school are a result of the kind of people admitted to study. Ewing writes,

> "The real source of stress is not the forced grading curve, not the work load, not the number of classes per week, but the students themselves. 'I think students put a lot of pressure on each other because of the kind of people we admit,' Dean John McArthur told the student newspaper. 'They're hard-driving, have high standards, and a lot of energy...' Moreover, the prevailing philosophy of the school is that pressure is not necessarily a bad thing. If these young men and women are to become top executives, they are going to feel a lot of heat in the business world. That being the case, it is best for them to get used to it and learn how best to cope with it. How they do that is up to them—no professor will attempt to tell them, for the answers vary with the individual. But in learning to do it, they will acquire an extremely important piece of know-how for succeeding as top executives....Time after time, alums tell me, the reason they didn't buckle when the economic battle got tough was that they knew how to deal with stress and applied what they knew out of habit. The habit, they acknowledge, was developed at HBS."[109]

Tough homework takes time and generates fatigue and frustration. Assigned thoughtfully, it stretches the student, stimulates self-learning that sticks, and ultimately, builds self-confidence. Stretch can turn to strain when there is regularly not enough time to get the work done, and not enough guidance, too much "figure it out for yourself." The bottom half or two-thirds of the class never gets closure, never "clicks" with the

---

[108] Cohen (1973) pages 80 and 86.
[109] Ewing (1990) page 52.

154

material. The ramp of assignments builds no self-confidence for them. Chapter 32 discusses setting work expectations for students. The *reasonably* tough instructor tailors high expectations to the developmental situation of the students, and aligns assignments to those expectations.

Classroom leadership

Reasonably tough discussion leadership draws students out directly (through the "cold call"), insists on fact-based or analysis-based recommendations, and challenges students to defend their ideas and derive deeper meanings or insights from the discussion. Students will experience a discussion-based class such as this to be intense, fast-paced, and possibly exhilarating. This leadership style becomes too tough with the addition of hazing, humiliation, bullying, and assertion that the student isn't working hard enough. Still, the tough instructor can gain high admiration from students. Robinson compared two instructors in Stanford's MBA program:

> "The scorn we heaped on Kemal, the ovation we awarded to Yeager—these say a lot about that fall term. Kemal was our age. He wanted to be our friend. But fall term was as traumatic for many of us as a war zone, and we didn't want a pal for a professor, we wanted a field marshal, someone we could rely on to tell us where we were going and then march us there. Yeager was cold and merciless and lived by the clock. But we knew we could rely on him, and by the end of the term we felt toward Yeager the way GIs felt toward Patton. We loved the bastard."[111]

Similarly, Reid describes a tough instructor at HBS:

> "This guy was a true hard-liner. In his class, chip shots would be taboo, and absences the kiss of death. He made this second policy unmistakably clear on the first day of class…It was quickly apparent that any vapid observation in Cooperman's class invited disaster. Our other professors had tended to let most comments pass with a nod or a brief editorial aside. Cooperman wasn't like this. He was more likely to interrogate students after they made a point, pushing their analysis further, and gauging how deep their understanding of the case went. His style bordered on confrontational, and intimidated a number of people. Not surprisingly, the man was an instant controversy in Section I. Many students walked out of the first class furious about his attitude and his modus operandi. I walked out exhilarated. 'This,' I said to anyone who'd put up with my

---

[111] Robinson (1994) page 105.

155

sermonizing, 'is how classes here were meant to be taught!' During his first session, Cooperman simply crucified three of the section's most prolific chip shot kings, leaving all of us squirming and cautious. We would have to think twice before tainting classes with subtle rephrasings of the obvious, and this would ultimately be to everyone's benefit…I would have preferred a business school swarming with Coopermans to one devoid of them. After all, the man could teach, and that's what we were there for…Discussion was enlivened further by his continued probing into the analysis of anyone who raised a point in class. Intimidating as this grilling could be, I still thought Cooperman's approach was the best of any of our professors to date. He elicited thoughtful and penetrating discussions, and kept the self-absorbed tedium of chip shots at bay."[112]

Arguments against being tough and demanding

There are many reasons to go easy. A casual survey of professional colleagues will yield a number of possible explanations for why they choose not to be tough, including the following:

- **"It invites confrontation."** Confrontation is risky, since it can head in lots of unanticipated directions. Confrontation is also emotionally hard, particularly if being a tough teacher is not consistent with the school's culture. Yet the ordinary day for most professionals is filled with confrontations, most of which go unnoticed. Taking the world on *its* terms can be just as risky as confronting it to consider your terms. Emotional support is indispensable for the tough teacher— here is where a mentor or seasoned colleague can help you think through the issues.

- **"Other instructors aren't tough, so why should I be?"** With the rising importance of teaching ratings at schools, instructors find themselves jockeying for competitive position. The untenured faculty member can be especially vulnerable to the need to win student acceptance, or at least not be caught at the bottom of the rankings. Here is where the *typical* behavior of other instructors becomes decisive: the impulse is to follow the crowd. Students sense this and can play instructors off against one another. Instructors who cave into this forsake two important professional anchors: their authenticity and their dedication to a field of knowledge.

---

[112] Reid (1994) pages 283-5.

- **"Other schools aren't tough, so why should our school be?"** This is the same ratings-oriented logic but now ratcheted up to the level of institutions. One hears this from students when a school dips a little in the magazine rankings. A fearful response by teachers and administrators simply moves the institution toward the mean of others, often sacrificing some of the special identity of the school and compromising its commitment to learning.

- **"Student self-esteem is paramount."** Surely one of the measures of an educated person is self-confidence about his or her mastery of a subject. But every teacher confronts false confidence in students, a kind of denial that asserts what one knows is good enough. The task of the teacher is to confront the false confidence as a first step toward building real confidence. In other words, constantly high self-esteem may not be consistent with genuine learning.

- **"I want to be liked, not feared or hated."** This is a fundamental need. But this assumes it is impossible to be tough *and* liked, or that once feared, always feared, or that the teacher has no one else from whom to gain support (such as family, friends, and professional colleagues).

- **"The students are adults.** They should be sufficiently self-motivated. Something is wrong if they need me (the teacher) to straighten them out. If there is a problem with this, take it to the Admissions Office." Whoa. The fallacy here should be obvious: the daily newspapers are full of professional fiascos in which bright, well-trained, well-informed *adults* failed spectacularly. Being an adult is no measure of perfection. Everyone can stand some correction.

- **"Our students are terrific: smart, well-trained, highly-motivated."** Or, "they are from the elite segment of society, on whose families our school depends for financial and social support. It would insult them to be tough and demanding." Just as with the previous point, the newspapers testify that intelligence and pedigree are no measure of mastery. Annually, most instructors witness the case of a bright student who coasts through a course, wanting academic credit, but unwilling to work very hard for it. This student needs clear feedback just as much as the worthy who works hard and excels.

- **"It's not in my job description or my paycheck.** Everyone knows that students come here just to get jobs. Why should I bother? Give me a break!" This is an attitude issue that is worthy of a separate discussion. For a start, see Chapter 37, "Ten Ideas for Long Term Development."

Profiles in too-tough: the "blowtorch" and the alien

A final argument against being tough is made by pointing to instructors who overdid it and left a trail of wreckage. The book, *Wittgenstein's Poker*, by David Edmonds and John Eidinow, helps define the outer boundary of "tough." It is the story of a famous 10-minute seminar attended by the three most eminent philosophers of the twentieth century, Bertrand Russell, Ludwig Wittgenstein, and Karl Popper, in which Wittgenstein grew angry at Popper, waved a fire poker at him, and then stormed out. The dispute sprang from a clash of ideas and personal styles. The authors describe Wittgenstein and Popper as follows: "Both were bullying, aggressive, intolerant, and self-absorbed…Like Wittgenstein, Popper tended to make his students feel useless."[113]

Popper displayed what Bryan Magee called "an intellectual aggressiveness such as I had never encountered before. Everything was pursued beyond the limits of acceptable conversation…In practice, it meant trying to subjugate people. And there was something angry about the energy and intensity with which he made the attempts. The unremitting fierce tight focus, like a flame, put me in mind of a blowtorch."[114] Another colleague called Popper an intellectual bully. Ivor Grattan-Guiness, a mathematician, said, "I thought his conduct was awful, frankly. He wasn't encouraging to students because he knew so much and he laid it on hard. Of course, this made you feel even more stupid than you were to start with. And the way he used to insult his own staff in front of students like me!"[115]

The assessment of Wittgenstein is equally startling. Iris Murdoch said, "[His] extraordinary directness of approach and absence of any sort of paraphernalia were the things that unnerved people. With most people you meet them in a framework, and there are certain conventions about how you talk to them and so on. There isn't a naked confrontation of personalities. But Wittgenstein always imposed this confrontation on all his relationships."[116] Peter Geach said, "[He] was brutally intolerant of any remark he considered sloppy or pretentious."[117] Stephen Toulmin said, "For our part, we struck him as intolerably stupid. He would denounce us to our faces as unteachable."[118] Edmonds

---

[113] See Edmonds and Eidinow (2001) pages 175-6 and 178.
[114] *Ibid.* page 176.
[115] *Ibid.* pages 177-8.
[116] *Ibid.* page 188.
[117] *Ibid.* page 190.
[118] *Ibid.*

and Eidinow wrote, "What crops up again and again in the many recollections of Wittgenstein is his power to arouse fear, whether in friend or foe."[119]

These are two tough cases, indeed, too-tough cases. They help us define the attributes of toughness run amok: aggressiveness, bullying, intense anger, intolerance. Edmonds and Eidinow attribute this behavior to high intelligence, egotism, unhappy childhoods, and exceptional drives to excel. At some schools, faculty behavior like this would bring the instructor before the Dean. This is plainly the dark side of being tough. Don't go there. And if you encounter it in instructors or students, intervene to help them change.

How tough to be? A positive case for the tough teacher

More than having good responses to the usual objections, one needs positive motives for teaching tough. Here it is: a passion for the quality of student learning. All of the very successful teachers I have known have been fairly tough. Their toughness is a signal to students about their own level of commitment to the classroom enterprise, to the discipline, and to the futures of the students. They believe that the signals about student mastery need to be clear or else (as price theory teaches) distorted signals produce aberrant behavior. They recognize that higher education socializes people for professional life. To prepare students for effective work and service in positions of leadership requires exposing students to the high expectations of professional life. And finally, tough teachers recognize that they are continually shaping a learning community, in which the teacher's responsibility is to defend the commons, the quality of joint discussion and work. In this setting, respect for the teacher's leadership is rarely just given; it is usually *earned* through a process of thoughtful and sincere demands on students and feedback on their performance.

The four quotations at the start of this chapter suggest aspects of this positive case. Jonson tells us that adversity *informs* one about strengths. The teacher is the informer, through the medium of structured assignments, classroom leadership, and grading. Langston Hughes's poignant poem reminds instructors of the responsibility to urge students onward: "Don't you set down on the steps/ 'cause you finds it kinder hard." Life *is* no crystal stair. Helping a student embrace that tough fact in an encouraging way is an enormous gift. The short story by Idries Shah suggests that an extremely important dimension of tough teaching is to reflect a large portion of responsibility for learning where it belongs: the student. The host blames Nasrudin for getting wet. Nasrudin's

---

[119] *Ibid.* page 201.

reply is priceless and tough: "Perhaps you did not contribute anything of your own to keeping dry?" And finally, Emerson reminds us that fear is a double-edged blade: an instructor of great sagacity and the herald of revolutions. In ancient texts, "fear" often means "deep respect." Such respect is a foundation of all learning: one must respect the lesson learned. But in its modern sense, fear can oppress (as with Wittgenstein and Popper) and impede learning. The successful tough instructor manages this duality very carefully.

Conclusion: How to be tough

How might the novice approach tough teaching?

1. **Leave your anger or other hang-ups some place far away.** They are extremely errant guides for any teaching style. Approach the teaching enterprise neutrally and respectfully. I believe that excellent teachers are distinguished by high self-awareness and self-regulation. These qualities figure into what Daniel Goleman describes as emotional intelligence.

2. **Meet students where they are, not where you want them to be.** This requires you to be well informed about the students, and where they are on the path of development. This is especially important if you teach in different arenas. An assignment that may be appropriate for doctoral students might be totally inappropriate for undergraduates.

3. **Give candid feedback** on assignments, in class, or in grades in ways tailored to the situation, and the student. *One size does not fit all.* This implies a coaching aspect to tough teaching. The news may be good or bad, but might be supplemented with a "Think about doing it this way next time…" Students who have been cold-called in class always welcome some kind of assessment, in the form of words delivered in person, by email, or hand-written note.

4. **Blend in a little warmth and humor.** Try smiling. Use wit. These help break the ice.

5. **Align any toughness to your own values.** If you have a hard time identifying the values relevant to a specific teaching situation, reflect on three questions. What kind of world do you want to live in? What kind of world do you want to create for your children? How would *you* like to be treated as a student in a similar situation?

Martin Luther King once said, "We must combine the toughness of the serpent and the tenderness of the dove: a tough mind and a tender heart." The challenge for student-centered teachers is similar.

Chapter 27
Gaining Closure

The instructor frequently hears questions from students that beg for *closure* to the class discussion. "So, what's the right answer?" "How did the case turn out?" "Where does this fit into the course?" From a teaching point of view, these are questions that most instructors have prepared answers for, at least to themselves, in the ordinary course of getting ready to lead a discussion. It would be easy to answer these questions. But, it may not really help to give students the kind of closure they seek—closure from the instructor might shortchange their chance to reflect and learn. Indeed, the questions may be a trap for both the instructor and the course. This chapter discusses why, and offers some suggestions for giving the right kind of closure.

The demand for closure

Students seek closure for a variety of reasons. First is a desire for efficiency: it takes less effort to be told than to figure things out for oneself. Second, ambiguity can be psychologically uncomfortable. The third has to do with the developmental stage of people in their third and fourth decades of life: they want to achieve and prove mastery. Objective closure to discussions is a way of checking mastery. Fourth, modern culture emphasizes ends over means, the arrival over the journey, the discovery over the search, the product (education) over the process (learning), *and answers over questions*. Fifth is a thirst for meaning, as if the student were to say, "I did all this work. Was it worth it?" These and other reasons exert a strong—almost gravitational—pull on the instructor to spill the beans and give a view, an outcome, an answer, or meaning.

How to close

Appetites are poor guides to needs. Remember the basic axiom: *one learns best that which one teaches oneself.* The primary consideration in deciding whether and how to give closure must be the promotion of the student's self-teaching. Done badly, closure might actually shut down self-teaching. Done well, closure can enrich student reflection and learning.

Closure that is student centered stimulates ongoing reflection and perhaps calls the student to action toward further exploration. A dangling question at the end of class can serve to promote thinking that becomes a foundation for the next discussion. Finally, if the energy of the class discussion seemed to pull students off-target from your learning objectives, a few well-placed words can begin the process of pulling them back on-target. Here are some guidelines:

- **Tailor closure to the needs of the student, and the opportunities of the course.** For example, short executive education programs are loaded with the objective signs of closure: minilectures, handouts, model solutions, etc. This is because executive education is generally more concerned with training than learning. In contrast, degree programs are *learning* experiences, i.e., longer, offering more opportunities to work with the student, and more focused on student self-discovery and making meaning.

- **Be proactive, not reactive.** Prepare in advance the closure *you* want to give and stick to it. This can pre-empt a lot of the lobbying for closure.

- **Be sparing.** A little closure goes a long way. Professors like to *profess;* once begun, it may be tough to rein in the temptation to tell everything one knows about the subject of that day. But doing so leaves little for student self-teaching. In addition, reconsider the belief that one must close every class, every day. The danger here is that once a routine is established, students will stop making their own notes, and instead will simply wait for the answer at the end of class. Vary the pattern and amount.

- **Don't run late.** A major challenge in closing any case discussion is to *leave enough time* at the end of class in which to give your comments. Once the class period ends, students' attention will melt away. If you run out of time, it is better simply to carry the closing comments over to another day than to drone on to a restless, distracted audience.

- **Attend to inflection points.** As the course moves from one general segment to the next, closure can help frame students' reflections on the classes already finished, and anticipate the classes to come. The retrospective can help students see linkages among classes and highlight open issues that are yet to be resolved in the forthcoming classes. Closure of this sort might be in the form of oral comments, or written notes that students could study later.

- **Motivate.** An important element of teaching is to encourage students forward in their learning. Closing comments are ideal moments for this encouragement, and could take many forms:

o *Cheerleading.* "This was a challenging class (or section of the course), and you did fine. Susan's comment was provocative and should stimulate us all to reflect on alternative solutions. Ben raised the contrast between this case study, and the company in the news yesterday: look for more comparisons."

o *Creating suspense.* "There is much more to the story here than meets the eye. We'll build on this in the next class. Until then, reconsider your key assumptions."

o *Emphasizing importance.* "Today's concept was the focus of the Nobel Prize for Economics in 1990. It radically changed practice, and became the springboard to newer discoveries."

- **Ask often, tell seldom.** The kind of closure that sets up ongoing student learning poses questions on which they can continue to reflect. At the most general, one can ask students to make their own closure with a question such as, "What did you learn today?" The answers, not always comforting, nonetheless lend clarity to the learning path of the students, and themselves create their own tension from which the next discussion can spring. I prefer closing questions that target more closely the learning objectives of the day. Here the objective is to take a teachable point, and turn it into a question for further reflection, to ask rather than tell. Consider two examples of telling and asking that set up very different kinds of closure for students:

Telling	Asking
"Water boils at 100 degrees Celsius."	"Does water always boil at 100 degrees Celsius? What do you think might be the effect of altitude, barometric pressure, or impurity (such as in sea water)? In short, what are the assumptions about the 100 degree 'rule'?"
"The stock market crashed in 1929."	"What made 1929's decline in stock prices a 'crash,' as opposed to a 'bear market'? Was this an isolated event in time and place, or was it linked to others?"

In closing

If there is an analogue to mindless learning, it is *mindless teaching*: teacher-centered, rote, seemingly definitive. Though this may be comforting to the student who wants outcomes without any process, it ignores the fact that very little within the span of human knowledge can be asserted simply and without qualification. To be educated means, among other things, to see and appreciate interesting variations, and *to teach oneself* on the basis of those variations. Closure can help this process; but often it frustrates it by suggesting too much definition to an indefinite world, and by choking off further reflection. The excellent teacher recognizes this, and employs closure very carefully, tailored to the student and the learning environment.

Chapter 28
Grading Class Contribution

Reflecting the vital nature of discussion to the student's learning, case method instructors typically allocate a large fraction of the final grade to the student's classroom contribution. As in an exam or term paper, the student demonstrates what he or she has learned, both before class, and in real-time during class. Grading serves to motivate student preparation, and afford feedback on the student's strengths and weaknesses. But in order to achieve any of these benefits, the process of grading class contribution must have *integrity*. This chapter outlines some important considerations.

Listening

Effective grading begins with effective listening in the classroom. Listening is a core skill of the student-centered teacher. To listen well, one must suspend preconceptions about the student, think like a learner, and *concentrate*. Paying close attention is a major task when one is leading a discussion at the front of the classroom—also on one's mind are one's own ideas, temperature, the rapid passage of time, chalkboard layout, and so on—observers will conclude that keeping track of what numerous students say is an impossibility. Yet one's capacity for recall *shortly* after class is better than might be thought. And with an appreciation for the kind of things one should listen for, the instructor can capture a lot of signal despite the noise. Here are some examples of what to listen for:

1. **Quality of ideas, analysis, and action recommendations.** This is the core demonstration of mastery. Given the challenges embedded in some teaching materials, it may not be possible for students to reach conclusions. But, one can ask them to talk knowledgeably about any analysis they did, why they did it, where their work halted, and what they would do next.

2. **Frequency of contribution.** My experience suggests that steady engagement in classroom discussion has a strong cumulative impact on learning. The effort of a student to participate regularly in discussion should be rewarded. The brilliant scholar who rarely participates, contributes little to the effort of the whole learning community—his occasional contributions may win some recognition under the first criterion (quality of ideas and analysis). But, his failure to help regularly will be recognized under this second criterion. At the other extreme is

the student who talks too much while contributing little of substance—this saps energy and denies better contributions to surface. In short, there must be a tradeoff between quality and quantity.

3. **Quality of process and argument.** The classroom community benefits when students direct their comments to the whole community, rather than just to the teacher. The ability to speak cogently about ideas and analysis offers further evidence of mastery. The use of humor and examples and the synthesis of other students' points into a larger argument help community learning and suggest that the student is making useful intellectual connections.

4. **Intellectual leadership/self-confidence.** The rare student displays real thought leadership. The teacher recognizes this in the body language and other indicators of respect when this student speaks. This student is there at important inflection points in the discussion, helping to deal with confusion, reframing the issues, and explaining.

Record keeping

Your ability to recall class contribution decays rapidly after class. *Immediately after leaving the classroom, the teacher should make some class contribution notes, usable later in grading.* A trick for making notes when you have back-to-back classes is to mark up a copy of the class seating chart with notes that could refresh your memory when you return to your office. For keeping formal records, one could create a standard format for information using a spreadsheet file on computer, with a student's record in each row, and the case or topic of the day in the column heading. Referring frequently to a seating chart and/or the student information cards, one could keep three kinds of notes on each student:

- **Numerical score** for class contribution that day. This ranges from '5' at the high end (for truly outstanding contribution), to '1' at the low (for students who say *something* even if only marginally useful). Occasionally, I award negative points to students who were disruptive or in some way significantly derailed the class.

- **Letter grade for any student who was 'cold-called'** to begin the class. The opening student might take up to 15 minutes to launch the case discussion this is a major opportunity to perform. The student will get points for the class, but also the letter grade, which is an important measure of quality.

- **Qualitative comments.** One could write brief comments on students' contributions each day in a column of the spreadsheet—these comments are cumulative across all classes. In my experience, these comments are the most difficult element to record (especially if one is tired after class), but they are also the most helpful basis for counseling students who are having difficulty in contributing to class discussions. And they are a trove of good material for stronger students who seek a letter of recommendation or your support on a scholarship application.

Monitoring progress

The virtue of spreadsheet-based class contribution records is that the instructor can easily monitor the progress of students over time, using averages or Z-scores[120] to measure their relative standing. In an environment of email, the instructor could easily offer some real-time feedback:

- Students who received a **negative evaluation** for that day deserve immediate and clear responses from the teacher. Class contribution should help a student; in the case of negative points, it *hurts* the student. The student needs to know the teacher's assessment, and to be counseled to turn around the behavior immediately.

- Students who received **high positive evaluation** for the day. Positive reinforcement always helps consolidate learning and classroom behaviors that can help others. In my experience, a little praise goes a long way. Don't overdo it, lest you create new problems of inflated self-esteem or trigger a relaxation response.

- Students with **low cumulative evaluation**. Starting about one-third of the way into the course, one could begin to identify students who are underperforming.

---

[120] A Z-score converts a raw contribution score for a student into the number of standard deviations from the mean for the entire class. Two-thirds of students in a normally distributed class will fall within plus or minus one standard deviation from the mean. Students with scores greater than +1.00 are in the top 15 percent of the students—and may be useful resources to call upon if a discussion is struggling. Those students with scores less than -1.00 are in the bottom 15 percent and may warrant some special feedback. The formula for the Z-Score is based on X, the contribution score for a particular student, X_M, the average score for the entire class, and SD, the standard deviation of scores for the entire class. The equation is $Z = (X-X_M)/SD$.

This is useful for keeping on the lookout for their contribution, and for offering some informal words of encouragement.

- Students who were **cold-called**. These are stressful experiences. A few words of encouragement, and suggestions for further thinking would help the student consolidate learning.

Grading

The virtue of spreadsheet-based class-contribution record keeping is the speed with which performance may be summarized at the end of the course. The point totals are easily summed, and converted to Z-scores. After ranking the students on the basis of these Z-scores, the hard judgment begins—here is where one should scrutinize the cold-call grades, the qualitative comments, and any *trends* in the quality or quantity of participation during the course. Of particular focus are any inconsistencies between numerical and qualitative assessments. Adjusting the ranking for fairness, one could look for clusters of performance as a possible basis for awarding letter grades. One needs to award the grades fairly, not only relative to the individual's performance but also with respect to the norms of the school. Resist any temptation to "send a signal" that is otherwise inconsistent with the facts of performance.

Conclusion

Grading that is based on careful listening, faithful recordkeeping, and an attitude of fairness has integrity. It gives reasonable feedback to the student about strengths and weaknesses and can highlight avenues for future growth.

Part 5
Handling Challenges From a
Student-Centered Point of View

Summary

This section addresses some outright traps for the novice and speed bumps for the experienced teacher. These are challenges because students may not play the role you hope they would for the discussion you want to have. Perhaps they don't talk. Or perhaps they challenge the teacher's fairness, workload, or professional credentials. Perhaps they hold an unfortunate grudge from past experience. Or even a major external tragedy may stagger the learning community. These chapters discuss possible actions, motivated by the philosophy of student-centered learning.

Chapter 29
When Students are Silent

Sooner or later, all case teachers face this difficult situation: the instructor asks a question, and no hands go up. Then, perhaps, the question is restated or rephrased, but still no response.   Students scrutinize their notes; there is no eye contact with the teacher. The instructor gets impatient and perhaps calls on a specific student to answer the question. The response is too brief, lacks energy. No other students take the cue. There is total silence. The discussion has stalled.

What to do in a situation like this will be dictated in part by its possible causes. Consider three types:

- **Day-specific** silence due to factors outside your course, but of short duration, such as fatigue (e.g., students just took an exam or handed in an important term paper), a breakdown of air conditioning on a summer day, and distraction (e.g., career placement activities or the spring fever of a beautiful day after a hard winter). In this first instance, students have not engaged the material, which is a problem of energy and motivation.

- **Material-specific** silence. Perhaps the case is long and confusing to the students. Or possibly students are not confident about the tools to be applied. Students are reluctant to make a public display of their confusion and lack of confidence. Superficially, the problem here is with the instructor's choice of material. Nevertheless, there can be sound pedagogical reasons for intentionally assigning challenging material, such as stretching the students' thinking, replicating confusion that may exist in the minds of practitioners, illustrating the state of the art, or, conversely, exploring the limits of analytical tools. To achieve these good ends requires that students talk about what they can and cannot do. When students are silent in this second instance, the root cause is the absence of risk-taking and of a classroom culture of candor.

- Silence arising from the **general learning environment** of the school. If you teach the only case course in a school at which the lecture method dominates, students may come to your course habituated to passive learning. Here, students will wait for the teacher to sort the case out for them and/or to present a model solution. At its worst, this can take on the dimensions of a supplier-customer relationship in which students will claim that since they paid for the course, it is the teacher (not the students) who should do the work. Thus, their silence ensues.

Of course, this environment flouts the Truth that one learns best what one teaches oneself. Indeed, the root cause in this third instance is the students' failure to take ownership for their own learning.

It helps to listen to students and to the school environment to detect the possible sources of silence. The response should be tailored to the probable source and reflect the gravity of the problem. Here is a menu of possible responses, in escalating priority:

1. **Ask your discussion question, and really wait.** It may be a difficult question on which students must reflect before replying. Remember that the silence probably feels as awkward for the students as for the instructor. Practice an expectant look; scan students for a sign of ideas; count silently to gauge how much time is passing. Too often, the instructor simply answers his or her own question (thus reinforcing students' tendency toward passive learning) or asks another question before students have had a chance to sort through the first one. Waiting is a special skill; it signals respect for the students' sorting-out processes, and implicitly demands that they (not the instructor) answer. Patience pays.

2. **Pause in your leadership of the case discussion and simply ask** the students, "What's going on?" This will expose any day-specific and material-specific problems. One instructor did so and learned that nearly half the students were walking flu cases and the other half had finished a mid-term exam the hour before. Asking students about their silence signals your interest in the students' side of the problem, and can energize the class. Of course, with public clarity about the students' problems, the instructor has an even sharper dilemma of how to respond: appearing to ease off in the face of weak excuses can create greater problems the next day. The next few responses form an intermediate level.

3. **Become more directive in your questioning.** This is a possible response to difficult material. Directive questioning looks for very specific responses and in effect walks the students along an analytical trail. The downside of directive questioning is that if used frequently, it can build a dependence on the instructor and reinforce passive learning.

4. **Buzz groups.** This is a useful response to day-specific problems of distraction and fatigue. One can stop the class and ask students to turn to the next person and take five minutes to discuss what they would do here... After a few minutes one can resume discussion by calling on a few students to present their ideas; usually more voluntary contributions follow quickly. In my experience, the buzz group has never failed to rejuvenate a flagging discussion. However, I avoid frequent use, lest the novelty wear off.

5. **Exhortation.** One can explain to students that discussion-based courses have a problem of the commons: if nobody contributes (i.e., if everyone "free rides") there will be no common intellectual capital from which to draw lessons. Everyone is better off if all participate actively. Students might be encouraged to ask questions if confused and above all to take risks: they can be reminded that there are rather few right answers in case analyses (though there are many wrong ones). Of course, the best placement for comments like these is at the beginning of the course, where they help frame the contract between students and instructor. Delivered in the middle of a course, the instructor must tailor the comments to the type of silence. To students who are fatigued or confused, comments like these can sound preachy or at worst, create resentments.

6. **Dismiss the class and ask for individual analyses to be turned in at the next class meeting.** One colleague did this and said, "I was amazed at what an electrifying effect that had on future preparation. Many students were highly complimentary of how that decision refreshed my discussions." This adds a sudden burden to the student workload, and can seem inconsiderate if students are under stress in other ways.

7. **Responses through course design.** These responses anticipate silence induced by the general learning environment. The instructor can tailor the incentive system to reward active participation. At Darden and Harvard, for instance, class contribution counts for up to 50 percent of a final grade. Also, the instructor can assign students to study groups specifically for the course. The aim here is to enhance daily preparation and give students a laboratory in which to test their ideas before facing the instructor. The syllabus of the course, and introductory comments by the instructor, should emphasize the importance (and requirement) of active contribution. The key point is that the implicit contract between students and instructor will strongly influence any propensity to silence. Again, the best time to implement a silence-fighting course design is at the beginning of the course.

There are other responses to silence, which I do *not* advocate. One is simply lecturing when the discussion stalls. Students quickly learn to quiet down and let the instructor do the work. Another is walking out on the students and agreeing to return only when they are ready to participate actively. A third is demanding that the students meet to discuss the case again (say, on Saturday afternoon, during the football game.) These latter two create resentments that make greater problems.

In conclusion, the instructor can view silence as a symptom of one or more barriers to learning. I have offered a menu of six useful responses to student silence. The artful instructor will tailor the response to the learning barriers.

Chapter 30
"You Haven't Given Me a Chance!":
Handling Objections That Question the Instructor's Fairness

A student comes to you to complain that she had her hand up to be recognized at several points in recent classes and was ignored by you. She believes that she missed, therefore, a number of opportunities to contribute to the discussion. Your course gives a material part of the final grade to class contribution. Thus, the student wants an opportunity to show what she can do. The tone and words of her comments suggest that you are unfair in your calling patterns. She wants "air time." How should you respond?

The appeal for more "air time"

This complaint is not unusual when highly motivated students mix with a grading structure that emphasizes contribution. Dealing with ebullient students presents special challenges. It would be easy to dismiss the student and her complaint. The student's message may contain a tinge of egotism and entitlement: "I deserve to be heard." To a busy instructor dealing with genuinely needy students, complaints like these invite a sharp response on the order of "Life is tough; keep trying." But the reality is that the alternative path of listening and coaching will almost certainly achieve better outcomes for the student, your classroom discussion, and your own case teaching style.

One's reply to the student could have the following components, and some inward reflections:

"Please be specific about what you think happened." Ask for the student's full story: specific instances, classes, segments of discussion. As a general rule in dealing with student complaints, it is important to get the student's perspective before responding. In addition, this models skills of listening, one of the most important attributes of an effective discussion teacher.

If you did not see the hand up, then reflect on your awareness of students' efforts to enter the discussion. In your calling patterns, try consciously to cover all students: front vs. back; left vs. right, men vs. women, domestic vs. foreign, introverts vs. extroverts, minorities, etc. While seeking diversity of contributors may seem artificial, students can tell you are trying to draw a broad cross-section of the class into the discussion and will respect the effort. Distributing your calling also helps you listen more effectively to the students. Asking a friend to observe your calling pattern can reveal blind spots. This way a colleague once discovered a bias against the extreme right-hand side of the classroom--I suspect that this is a common bias for right-handed instructors who, as they turn from writing on the chalkboard, see first and call on the students on the left and center of the room. Generally, an important technique is to pause for a second or two before calling on a student, in order to survey the full range of choices before you. You could also move around the room to get different perspectives on the calling opportunities. Doing so, you'll cover your blind spots and make more thoughtful calling decisions.

If you saw the hand up, acknowledge that you saw it. This helps address the student's sense of neglect and signals that you are aware of the student's effort to contribute. It also signals that you consciously chose to pass the student by--here is an important opportunity for you to coach the student about the culture of the case method classroom. One set of comments might reflect the fact that the discussion leader needs to choose contributions that build the discussion toward the goals for the day. This may entail letting one student talk at length to develop a complex idea, or returning repeatedly to a few advocates or debaters. The very important idea here is that the instructor must be a leader, not just a traffic director.

Another set of comments to the student might reveal what you think of the student's contributions to date, and how your assessment of the student possibly influenced your decision to pass her by. It might simply be a student you've heard a great deal from in recent classes. "I know you have a lot to say here, but I needed to open up the discussion to let other students contribute." It might be that based on your earlier observations of the student, you have concluded that she does not listen very well to the discussion and therefore derails its flow: "you tend to respond to issues that we covered earlier in the class" or "you tend to offer pre-prepared remarks, rather than what will advance the discussion toward its goals." Sometimes students can get defensive about your assessment, so try to use phrases that are coaching, rather than adversarial. I have seen major improvements in students' discussion skills following a conversation like this, so don't shrink from the opportunity to give feedback.

Of course, you could have passed her by for reasons other than for the good of the discussion: your own fatigue, distraction, or bias. These can erode the most effective case leadership styles and need to be managed actively. Part of what we owe students is our objectivity and alertness. Sometimes a student's complaint is a useful wake-up call.

In closing a conversation like this, one could solicit the student's help in two ways. First, "Trust me to do the right thing." It may sound corny to ask this, but trust is crucial to the success of the case classroom. For the sake of their own learning, students must believe in the case discussion leader and case discussion process. It never hurts to ask. Second, "Please help me build the kind of classroom culture that achieves the big goals: we need to hear from lots of people; the comments need to be appropriate to the flow at the time; we need good ideas backed by solid analysis; and we need a willingness to take risks and challenge our thinking." Closed this way, the meeting reflects some responsibility back onto the student for the success of the enterprise.

A conversation about "air time" is an opportunity for leadership, to model good qualities of the discussion leader, and to convey one's vision for an effective class.

Chapter 31
"If You Are So Smart, Why Aren't You Rich?"
And Other Brash Questions to the Teacher

The new term begins. You introduce yourself, describe the course, and pause to invite questions before starting to teach. It's a moment of buoyancy; you're ready to begin work. Then a student asks a brash question. "What qualifies you to teach this course?" Or "Have you personally done any of the deals (financings, investments, etc.) this course covers?" Or "Have you worked in this industry?" Or, "Do you consult in this area?" Or, "What practical work experience do you have?" Or the showstopper, "If you're so smart, why aren't you rich?" A stillness falls over the room as everyone recognizes that a not-so-subtle challenge has been issued. If you are a newly minted Ph.D., there may not be much work experience to discuss. Or as a senior professor, your work experience may not be quite that relevant or recent. You are on the spot to justify your presence. You briefly contemplate a response that is comparable in rudeness to the query.[121] But instead you search for the right words. What should you say?

This would be an amusing vignette except that my conversations with numerous instructors suggest that these kinds of questions have grown more common in recent years. And they are serious events. The instructor's response will set a tone that echoes throughout the entire course and perhaps shows up in the final evaluations. The incident and the possible responses say a lot about the fundamental challenges an instructor faces in gearing students to become their own best teachers.

Behind the brash question

Underlying the question are notions that reveal a fundamental misunderstanding of the learning enterprise, a quest for control, and a search for meaning. Any effort to respond to the question must be rooted in an understanding of these issues.

First, the question implies that the instructor determines the quality of the learning experience. But instead, the classroom process—especially where cases are discussed—is much more like a community experience. Everyone bears responsibility. It is the role of the instructor wisely to frame questions and shape the engagement with important

---

[121] I have it on reliable authority that Nobel Laureate Merton Miller replied to the brash question with an equally brash response, "If *you're* so rich, why aren't you smart?"

ideas. From a student-centered point of view, it would be equally appropriate for the student to have asked the other students what kind of learners they are.

Second, the question embeds a challenge to the instructor's control. "Who is in charge here?" the student seems to ask. Fashionable among many degree students is the idea that they are customers and that the school is a supplier. Business schools teach the primacy of customers. Therefore students assume that their expectations must govern. Of course, one good metaphor deserves another: perhaps students are merely work-in-process inventory ultimately to be consumed by the businesses, governments, and society that need their skills—this would imply that they are to be marched without murmur toward graduation. For instructors who derive some energy from their students, this is not a very appealing model. I prefer a third metaphor: partners. The truth is that instructors and students really need each other and need a high level of cooperation in order for the learning enterprise to sparkle. Instructors need to listen to students the way any sharp businessperson would listen to a market. Under the partner view, the instructor is an artful leader; students are thinking, responsive followers. Students must let teachers lead.

Third, even affirmative responses to the question ("Yes, I have done those deals, worked many years, and above all, am rich") would imperfectly predict the quality of learning that the student will experience. The skills that enable one to do very well in a particular line of business or finance may map poorly on the requisites necessary to teach well. That some students might care more about business credentials than about learning suggests that it is still true that a prophet has no honor in his own village.

Fourth, the question betrays a degree of incredulity or mistrust in the educational process. This may be a sign of the times. Consumer research, for instance, on "Generation X" suggests that consumers born since 1965 are less brand-loyal and more transaction-oriented, that is, much more careful to scrutinize whether value received equals or exceeds the price in this transaction (i.e., class session, or course).[122] Baby boomers, and their parents, are much more relationship-oriented, more prone to trust that through repeated engagement with a brand (a professor, a curriculum, or a school), value received will equal or exceed price. If one trusts the process, then one is likely to believe that across a variety of courses and classes the education will indeed come together. But if one demands no downside variance at every transaction, then one becomes a tough customer.

---

[122] For a sampling of this research, see Karen Ritchie, *Marketing to Generation X* Lexington: Lexington Books, 1995, and J.W. Smith and A.S. Clurman, *Rocking the Ages: The Yankelovich Report on Generational Marketing*, New York: HarperBusiness 1998.

Finally, the question is motivated at least in part, by a desire for meaning. The student seems to ask, "Will the hours of preparation, the personal denial necessary to get through the work, the group projects, quizzes, and exam all make sense? Will all this prepare me to become something I want to be?" The instructor could say, "Probably yes." But ultimately no direct response offers much comfort. By focusing on the instructor's credentials, the student is seeking some added assurance that the experience will be meaningful. I think this angst is the heart of the problem. As a result, the good news is that the instructor should never take the rude question personally. The bad news is that making meaning takes a lot of effort and careful thought. Ultimately one cannot make meaning for the students; they must make it themselves.

Responding

From an understanding of the drivers of the question, one can begin to craft a response. Above all, neither avoid the question, nor attack the questioner. The question is telling you something; view it as information. Also, view this as an opportunity to meet a challenge and assert your intellectual command of the classroom. I think that the best response to the question about credentials consists of some or all of the following:

1. A direct question deserves **a direct answer**. One can reply describing one's degrees, research in the area, work experience and private consulting, and one's years teaching. My strong advice is to keep this short—refer the students to your website, for instance, for more detail on your work and C.V. Your basic argument must be, "I've had X years of intense study in this area and have a lot of insights to offer." But the more time you spend describing your credentials, the more you legitimize the wrong focus. For most Ph.D.s, keeping it short will not only be desirable, but a necessity.

2. **Tone and delivery** count for a lot here: you (and no one else) are in charge in this classroom. If necessary, a little practice in front of a mirror will help you develop a voice and demeanor that will convince the student that you really mean business. Also, watching a seasoned colleague's delivery often affords an invaluable model.

3. Remind the students that your **course is a community**, an educational enterprise for which the success rests on the shoulders of all. The instructor will play an important role, not the least of which is to demand steady and high performance for the good of the commons. Indirectly this says that it is not the instructor's credentials that matter so much, as the effort and quality of interaction of all.

What you could say is "Everyone in this room brings different experiences and strengths, which our discussion process harnesses to solve *real problems*. We should focus on how *we all* work together to focus on these problems."

4. If useful, you could segue into comments about the possible **importance of your course to a student's professional development**. The subject may be foundational to a variety of pursuits, or a gatekeeper for students seeking to enter a specific career. The topic area may be especially timely in light of current events. Specific skills gained in the course may assist students in professional exams. Aspects of the course may help explain mysterious behavior of managers or organizations. All of these points may have been made in your syllabus, but one can confidently expect that most of the students will not have absorbed those points before the start of the course. The instructor simply needs to **sell the relevance of the course and learnings**.

By the end of your response, you have spent 20 percent of the time talking about yourself, and 80 percent of the time talking about the relevance of the learning experience and how to make it a success. If one believes that meaning and command are the key issues, then this is probably the right balance.

5. **Start the discussion process soon.** Discussion is engaging and is its own best sales device. Dwelling at length on the first four points makes you seem defensive and digs into a deeper hole. *Just get started:* "What are the problems in this case, and what would you recommend?

The richness of the teacher

In a series of superb essays, the economic historian, Donald McCloskey, addressed the brash question, "If you are so smart, why aren't you rich?" He argued that the role of the scholar and critic is entirely different from the role of the entrepreneur; the role of the scholar is to hold a mirror up to society that it might know itself better. McCloskey wrote:

> Harry Truman had it about right. The expert as expert, a bookish sort consulting what is already known, cannot by his nature learn anything new, because then he wouldn't be an expert. He would be an entrepreneur, a statesman, or an Artist with a capital A. The expert critic can make these non-expert entrepreneurs more wise, perhaps, by telling them about the past. But he must settle for low wages.

Smartness of the expert's sort cannot proceed to riches. Economics teaches this.[123]

Most university instructors I know aren't *rich* in the sense of Bill Gates or Warren Buffett. Those fortunate enough to get tenure gain a financial commitment that in present value terms is sizable. Some faculty members, particularly those in the professional schools, consult on the side. But by and large instructors lead merely comfortable, middle-class lives. Teaching, however, creates riches of a different sort:

- **Satisfaction** of mastering a complex subject and stimulation from the challenge of maintaining that mastery as the subject evolves over time.

- **Delight of the "Aha!"** Seeing the look of recognition in a student's eyes as he or she grasps an idea is, for me, one of the enduring gifts from teaching.

- **A sense of being part of something larger.** One trains people to work in the world and make things better. As time passes, you learn of a few students who have stumbled, though most have actually made a positive difference in the world. John Dewey said that the barbarian is only a generation away—but for the work of teachers, society would be considerably worse.

The riches of teaching are relatively well hidden from students and, I think, do not belong at the opening of a course or a response to a brash question. They remain a source of private motivation through what can be a trying confrontation with students.

Conclusion

The brash question is difficult to answer *directly* in ways that will be satisfying to the student. The instructor's credentials (i.e., smarts and/or riches) are the wrong foundation for making meaning of the educational experience. The best response is to deal with the underlying drivers of the question: misapprehensions about the learning process, a quest for control, and ultimately, meaning about the struggle to teach oneself.

---

[123] Donald N. McCloskey, *If You're So Smart: The Narrative of Economic Expertise*, Chicago: University of Chicago Press, 1990, page 134.

Chapter 32
"'Professor, How Much Work Do You Expect Me To Do?'
-- Setting Expectations for Class Preparation"

The question, ("How much work...?") arises at inopportune moments and carries shadings of complaint, rebuke, resistance, and negotiation from the student. You may be just launching the course. Or perhaps the course has entered a stretch of heavy lifting. Or the students need to extend their reach in order to grasp a great idea. You size up the student and see a novice who is thrashing about, or a gifted amateur-type who feigns indifference about making an effort, or a budding education theorist who argues that "less is more,"[124] or a night-school student who is juggling job, family, and education. Perhaps the student points to the supposedly low level of work required in the course next door (or the course last year or at another school) as a benchmark for how much one should prepare in your course now. You have made a reasonable effort to align the workload of the course with the course credit, but the question suggests you failed. You value education through self-learning, but the student seems to want to get it on the cheap. You remember the long lonely self-preparation of doctoral studies, or some take-no-prisoners experiences of professional life: negotiating for relief was not a possibility, and complaint would land you on the street. You want to remain in control of your own course and resent the attempt to bargain for a revision in terms. You would love to ignore the question, but can't. How you respond has big implications since decent student preparation is the *sine qua non* of a successful class and course.

First, don't overreact. Any challenging course will ventilate student grief. Muzzle not the ox as he treadeth out the grain, and certainly don't feel that you must give the ox a shady berth from which to contemplate the grain from afar. An important role of the professor is to structure the educational journey. Reflect on why you chose these assignments. They were probably motivated by a reasonable view about what is important and how students learn best. The payoff of learning through self-discovery is huge. Solid preparation amplifies the learning in class. As Louis Pasteur said, "In the fields of observation chance favors only the prepared mind." By demanding preparation, the instructor is helping students get lucky—and to learn.

---

[124] To the contrary, less could be less, as illustrated by the fact that if you don't prepare at all, you won't learn much. And surely one does not become *more ignorant* with more preparation. But past a certain point there may be diminishing returns to spending more time on preparing for class. The key judgment for the instructor is to assess that point of diminishing returns.

Second, learn from the question. It offers some data about your course and your teaching, so it is worthwhile to mine it for insights about the student, this next assignment, and/or the course.

- **The student.** Perhaps if one student screws up the courage to ask this question, there are others who feel the same way. Without a systematic survey, you will never know for sure. But the identity of the questioner offers some clues. What can the attributes of this person tell you about how the workload of the course is being experienced, and by whom?

- **The assignment and its context.** A complaint about any task is relevant only in some setting, defined by available time, resources, distractions, and alternatives. It is worth reflecting *again* on the size of the task you have imposed on the students. Out of one's own enthusiasm for the subject, it is easy to assign too much preparation. The polar alternative is to so extensively summarize and distill that you remove all nuance and contingency from the subject. Most self-taught instructors will err on the side of too much (trusting in their own enthusiasm) rather than too little. The context also plays a huge role in whether an assignment is perceived to be burdensome. Intense job placement periods, homecoming weekends, school conferences, and the like have a way of turning the most reasonable assignments into burdens. When you designed the course, were you alert to the impact of the context? To what other upcoming context demands should you attend?

- **The course.** A question of workload coming at the start of the course may be a signal about student uncertainties ("If I work this hard, will I get a commensurate return?") and about the reputation of the course. Have you clearly articulated a value proposition to students about your course? A question later in the course, that does not seem tied to a specific student, assignment, or context, may well be a challenge for control. What is it about the course, the students, or you that raises control issues now?

One should be reluctant to act hastily or make major changes in assignments in the middle of the course on the basis of these insights. But they certainly should help calibrate your course design and assignments in the next offering.

Third, reflect on the instruments through which you can shape student expectations about preparing for class:

- **Your words.** At the start of the course, you must be clear about how class preparation helps the entire class, the quality of discussion, and one's individual grades. A little cheerleading may be useful, but the basic tone must be a demand motivated by a vision that will appeal to the student. Also, it helps to frame for the students what it means "to be prepared" to discuss a case study or class assignment. You might suggest that preparation consists of (a) a recommendation, b) some analysis to back up the recommendation, and c) questions or next steps that the student might pursue if he or she had more time.

- **Your actions.** In class, you might compliment a student who is obviously well prepared and helps make the class a success. Students who are obviously unprepared could be cold-called, confronted, and reminded that daily preparation is essential to their learning. Before or after class, you might coach selected students about their preparation. Occasionally, one could drop in on study teams with words of encouragement and advice. All these actions signal to students the importance of preparation.

- **A written trail.** Your course syllabus should state explicitly that daily preparation is expected and will have a material effect on one's learning and grades. You might send notes or emails to well-prepared and under-prepared students—a little of this goes a long way to influence the word-of-mouth reputation about your course. And finally, you might distribute some written comments on what it means to prepare well—in this regard, see Chapter 24 "Shaping the classroom contract: How the teacher might brief the student about preparing for a case method class."

Distilling all of these elements into an on-the-spot reply to the "How much..." question might suggest a response as follows:

I expect you to come to class each day, prepared to discuss the case. This means you should have a decent grasp of the facts in the case; you should have completed some analysis (usually quantitative) in response to the advance assignment questions; and you should have some recommendations for action, suitable for presentation to the protagonist of the case. I think you can do this in an average of 2.5 hours per class—this assumes an hour and a half for your personal preparation of the case, plus an hour for a study team discussion. If you can't wrap up the case in 2.5 hours, then I expect you to bring to class a grasp of the facts of the case, some clarity about where and why you ran aground, and what you would do next if you had more time—a steady habit of this is not good, but I'll assume you are adults and will make wise judgments in response to circumstances. Coming to class totally unprepared and without extenuating circumstances is equivalent to an unexcused absence and will adversely affect your class contribution grade. My course syllabus, posted on the website and well known to you, says all this and discusses the relation between preparation, contribution, and grading. The assignments are manageable and will make you strong professionals. I think you can do it. Go for it!

A response such as this, delivered directly and without preaching, signals high expectations, the seriousness of your intent, and the fact that you are in charge and cheering them along. But it also sets realistic time targets and acknowledges that the student has some choice in the matter. In the final analysis, there is no substitute for clear expressions of the need for students to prepare for class. Find your own way to express this, and then do not hesitate to do so. Your students depend on it.

Chapter 33
Tragedy as a Teachable Moment

Everything about teaching has to do with making meaning for oneself, and encouraging students to make their own meaning. One makes meaning both through "what one says" and "what one does." Tragedy can stifle meaning—both in the ordinary learning enterprise, and about the tragedy itself. A dramatic example of this would be the terror attacks of September 11, 2001. These interrupted educational life and cast a pall that lasted for months. Schools are more familiar with the effect of local tragedies. Events such as fires, suicides, crimes, and accidents periodically savage the learning focus of a school. All of us who lead in any way—managers, parents, professors— struggle with what to do and say in the face of tragedy. How can one promote meaning-making and restore the learning enterprise?

Making meaning through what one does

Most tragedy that affects the learning enterprise happens at some distance of the classroom, denying leaders the opportunity to be there. Yet instructors have a range of action across which they could make meaning through doing:

- **At school: be visible.** In one's own personal grief, it is easy to withdraw. But what students need is the presence and engagement of their educational leaders. *Be there* even when you don't know what to say. Sometimes talk is useless; but listening will be vital.

- **With students and colleagues: show empathy.** Simple expressions that you share the grief of students are important. The greatest impact of such expressions is probably one-on-one.

- **In your course: create slack.** Adapt your requirements in proportion to the nature and extent of the tragedy. Adhering rigorously to due-dates of papers, practices of cold-calling, etc. may place you on a collision course with students (and administrators). Canceling class may be warranted if the event is severe.

- **Attend to yourself.** Helping others can promote your own efforts to make meaning. But the stress of the tragedy may intrude on your life in hidden ways. After September 11th, executives reported depression, loss of sleep, and other indicators of the stress of trying to lead in a time of tragedy. One chief executive officer told me that he formed a group of peers to discuss ways of coping personally with the stress. However you do it, you should look for resources to help yourself.

Making meaning through what one says

It is possible for tragedy to be a teachable moment. I believe there are at least four teaching points in tragedy, to be spoken in individual conversations, small groups, and even in class. These are obvious and yet so easily obscured that they bear repeating, in large and small ways, by those who teach, directly or even indirectly:

- **The world is a dangerous place.** Safety nets can fail. Security systems can be circumvented. Volatility is all around us. Behavioral scientists report that humans tend to oversimplify risk. They extrapolate an historical growth trend into the future. They tend to think tomorrow will be rather like today. They filter and ignore anomalies. They cling to comfortable stereotypes and frameworks. To understand that the world is a dangerous place is to remember that the world varies from these comfortable heuristics, to study risk in all its forms, to hedge in sensible ways, to remain agile, and to prepare even for the worst.

- **The importance of leading from where you are.** The single most direct means of making meaning in the face of tragedy is to *act.* The stories of immediate response to the terror attacks of September 11 are assertions of life in the face of death. To stare tragedy down is an extraordinary act of making meaning. The stories emerging from the scenes of tragedy give numerous examples of people who became leaders on the spot by virtue of the fact that they were there, perhaps had a little more clarity about the possibilities than others, and somehow found the words to energize others about those possibilities. The virtue of leading from where you are is central to the widespread transformation of business enterprise that began in the mid-1980s. We probably expect too much of "official" leaders. They rely on the rest of us in smaller settings to take up the common cause.

- **One can (and must)** *choose* **a view and an attitude.** In his classic book, *Man's Search for Meaning,* Viktor E. Frankl reflected on his experience in a Nazi concentration camp: "Everything can be taken from a [person] but one thing: the last of the human freedoms—to choose one's attitude in any given set of circumstances, to choose one's own way." [125]   To make meaning in a tragic world

---

[125] Victor E. Frankl, *Man's Search for Meaning,* 4th ed. Boston: Beacon Press, (1959, 1984, 1992) page 75.

begins with the realization that one can *choose* how to engage that world. Frankl wrote,

> *What was really needed was a fundamental change in our attitude toward life. We had to learn ourselves and, furthermore, we had to teach the despairing men, that <u>it did not really matter what we expected from life, but rather what life expected from us.</u> We needed to stop asking about the meaning of life, and instead to think of ourselves as those who were being questioned by life—daily and hourly. Our answer must consist, not in talk and meditation, but in right action and in right conduct. Life ultimately means taking the responsibility to find the right answer to its problems and to fulfill the tasks which it constantly sets for each individual.* [126]

It is easy to dismiss tragedy as "stuff happens." But this is a form of denial that does nothing to prepare one for leadership. We are necessarily in the world; but we can choose whether we want to be *of* the world, whether we allow the prevailing conditions to define who we are. Professionals necessarily make choices. To "have a view" is to have an outlook about the future and a mind-set about what matters. Professionals are not agnostic toward the drivers of events. Nor are they fatalists. They have an attitude, a stance about whether and how to act on their view. One's attitude is an action plan of sorts.

- **Courage is the cardinal virtue.** The remarkable stories that emerged from the terror remind us that there remains an unspoken dimension to leadership and the preparation of professionals. What makes it possible to struggle and lead in a dangerous place? I believe it was C.S. Lewis who said that courage is the cardinal virtue because it *makes all other virtues possible.* Much of what we do in professional life should seek to build courage in (to *en*-courage) others because of the enormous multiplier effect it has on other things they do. All courage derives from faith in something, and drives out fear. Martin Luther King Jr. used to recite the poem:

> Fear knocked at the door.
> Faith answered.
> There was no one there. [127]

---

[126] *ibid.* page 85.
[127] Quoted in Darlyne Bailey, "The Power of Dialogue," in *Researchers Hooked on Teaching,* Thousand Oaks, CA: Sage Publications, page 302.

Thus, to encourage others one must build their faith—this is what is meant by the assertion that true leaders *make meaning*.

- **Celebrate heroes.** In post-modern American culture it has not been fashionable to discuss heroes or heroism. It is said that all heroes have flaws, that heroism is not an absolute but rather is situation-specific, and that heroes diminish self-esteem of the rest of us. Each criticism bears a grain of truth, but in sum they get the perspective completely wrong. We should celebrate heroes not because of who they are, but because of who *we* can become, and the meaning we hope to make. Exemplars are among the most important vehicles available to teachers. The stories of heroism that emerge out of tragedy enliven all of us as to our own potential to make meaning in the face of nihilism, to find courage where there is fear, to lead in the small as well as the large, to struggle even to the point of the ultimate sacrifice, and to live with dignity in a dangerous world. The poet, Stephen Spender, said it best:

> *"I think continually of those who were truly great...*
> *The names of those who in their lives fought for life,*
> *Who wore at their hearts the fire's center.*
> *Born of the sun, they traveled a short while towards the sun,*
> *And left the vivid air signed with their honor."*[128]

---

[128] Stephen Spender, "I Think Continually of Those Who Were Truly Great," in *Treasury of Favorite Poems*, Louis Untermeyer (ed.) New York: Barnes & Noble Books, 1996, page 574.

Part 6
And furthermore...

Overview

This final part of the book ties up some open issues, sketches some paths for ongoing instructor development, and lends some summary of main points in the book. In particular, you will find

- **Reflections** on the three cases about Henry Domhoff (Chapter 2), Elizabeth Kent (Chapter 3), and Eduardo Mendez (Chapter 4). Recall that these three mini-case studies were offered as exercises at the beginning of the book, against which to gauge the evolution of your thinking. Here at the end, I offer my own comments on the three cases, as a way of stimulating a conversation with your own teaching muse. While there are no definitively "right" solutions to most case studies, there may be many wrong ones. I trust that you will find my comments to be right enough.

- **Suggested paths** that can stretch and strengthen one's teaching skills. I believe that one never finally "arrives" at being a good discussion leader; one is always developing. Chapter 37 ("Ten Ideas for Long Term Development") aims to help you think beyond the next class or the next semester.

- **Summary** of main ideas and suggested **"next steps."** Chapter 38 offers an overview of the teaching suggestions surveyed in this book, and suggests ways of implementing and revisiting them.

Chapter 34
Reprise of Chapter 2: Henry Domhoff[129]

Henry's course opener is a real baptism by fire. Like watching an automobile crash in slow motion, Henry's first reaction is surprise. The full impact of the event will occur quickly, and it won't be pretty. This is a serious event in the life of a course, and the reputation of a teacher. How the instructor responds sets expectations and tone for the learning experience of students. And it may well reappear in the student evaluations at the end of the semester. Henry's contract is up for renewal; he could surely use a boost in his teaching ratings in this course.

Henry's chief problem is the rather direct challenge to his authority at the head of the classroom. Questions about relevance and authority are tough to answer. This is not a polite "Tell us about yourself" query; it is openly sarcastic. It implies that he is poor and therefore unrespectable—to respond directly would require Henry to prove a negative, rather like the unfortunate politician confronted by a journalist who asks, "When did you stop beating your spouse?" Chapter 31 suggests that such challenges to authority have several roots:

- Misunderstanding of the learning enterprise. In the case method classroom, everyone bears responsibility for success of the enterprise. More deeply, a challenge probably suggests a mistrust of the learning process, a sentiment that survey research suggests may have generational roots.

- Consumerism. Students, and some school administrators, liken students to customers. If the customer is always right, then students will infer that the learning experience must be structured to make it pleasurable for them. They seem to say, "I'm the customer, do it my way." This implies disrespect for the judgment of the instructor: a prophet who has no honor in his own village.

- The mere cosmetics, and the actual fact, of an instructor's base of authority to teach a subject. Henry is young and has no work experience in the area of the course. His specialty is actually in a different area: derivatives. Did the Dean's Office make the right choice in appointing Henry to teach this subject? Was Henry wise in accepting the assignment? Once the decision was made, how did Henry and the Dean rationalize the appointment to students?

---

[129] I thank Professor James Gentry and seminar participants at the 2001 Financial Management Association meetings for several insights raised in a discussion of this case.

- A desire for meaning. Will all this make sense? Will this prepare me to become something I want? Chapter 9 discusses meaning-making.

Laughter among students suggests that the challenge of the questioner is not isolated; one must infer that others in the room share the sentiment. And finally, this challenge has the qualities of a *tipping point* where an assessment of the teacher and course either spread broadly, or get stopped (see Chapter 25 about the spread of ideas). Henry needs to respond effectively, right now.

One must question Henry's *attentiveness* to the learning process and the audience. He arrived at the classroom with only two minutes to go before the start of class, leaving no time to read the mood of students, prepare himself for teaching, and make personal contact with the audience. Chapters 6, 12, and 15 discuss making contact with students. Henry ignored the restlessness of students as he droned on about administrative matters— all of which were covered in the printed syllabus that students had received in advance. And his surprise at the unfolding incident ("This isn't starting the way I wanted") raises the question of how Henry *did* want it to start. It is one thing to have some comments for the day outlined, and another to envision how the class must contribute to the entire semester-long learning experience.

There may be some aspects of *school culture and environment* that contribute to the event. Are students this disrespectful to all instructors? If so, why wasn't Henry prepared? If not, why is Henry singled-out for this experience? Note that students continued to arrive late well after the start of class—is this too a sign of disrespect for the learning process, or just a fact of life for students who are commuters and must deal with a faulty mass-transit system?

In sympathy to Henry, course openings are loaded moments for students and teachers. This is the point at which an implicit contract gets struck that defines roles, work expectations, and desired outcomes. Chapter 24 discusses the classroom contract. Had Henry adequately prepared for using this class to best advantage? If so, then why didn't he focus on motivations and a fundamental value proposition for students?

In response to this multidimensional problem, consider possible actions over three ranges of time:

- **Right now.** Henry might answer the question directly, but he needs to use his answer as a way to shape students' expectations in a useful direction. It is not sufficient to discuss degrees, research, and other work experience; based on what we know about Henry's background, he won't win the contest on that terrain. He might mention his training and teaching experience quickly, but then he must move quickly to do the following:

- **Assert the value proposition of the course.** Many challenges to leadership are simply challenges about meaning of the effort. Henry needs to start making meaning by suggesting ways in which the course can pay off for students. These might include professional preparation, admission to higher-level courses, preparation for important exams (CPA, GRE, CFA), learning how to apply concepts from other courses, and simply having a stimulating experience. Students from "Generation X" tend to be tough customers and will tend to buy-in if the transaction seems beneficial. Henry needs to sell the value potential of the course in a way that appeals to the hearts and minds of students, and goes well beyond a recitation of the course details in the syllabus.

- **Sketch the roles and work necessary to deliver that value.** Here's the point of heavy lifting: the value will be delivered if everyone forms a learning community, and follows Henry's lead. He can't *prove* that the value will be delivered; the students must *trust* him and the learning process. Students must prepare for each discussion, and then participate. Henry's job is to structure the work and lead the discussions to solid learning. Henry can point to the fact that this method works, as suggested by long history of, and current pervasiveness of discussion-based teaching like this. All of these are positive selling points. In some situations, Henry might even use a negative point: students who are strongly skeptical should opt-out right now and let those who really want to learn build the community that is necessary. Of course, this only works if students have a choice. And the tough attitude it suggests might push more students over the edge and out of the classroom. Erosion in enrolments might hurt Henry in the eyes of the Dean's Office.

- **Take charge.** Henry needs to get his message across in a self-confident and even assertive fashion. Without the other lofty theories about why this is happening, it is almost certain that the students are doing what students have done for millennia, testing the responses of the instructor. At the ending point of the case, Henry seems flustered. He should step out from behind the podium, and even walk up the aisles as he delivers his points in strong volume. Eye contact is vital, especially with those students who challenged him. He should *not* invite further discussion of his qualifications to teach the course—this has to be a take-it-or-leave-it point beyond which Henry is going to teach and not sacrifice more valuable time for a discussion of it.

o **Get into a discussion of the case as soon as possible.** What sells students on the discussion method or any particular teacher are the *sense of engagement, and the effectiveness* of the method. If Henry wants to win over the wavering middle of the class, he needs to employ his biggest weapon, the method itself. To help him assert command, he could cold-call a student—a risky tactic if the students are unprepared. Henry could repeat the assertion of student contribution and preparation. If everyone is unprepared, he should stop the class, require that they read the case there, and resume with an abbreviated discussion later.

- **For the rest of the course.** Starting with the next class, and running into following classes, Henry needs to reinforce norms of preparation, participation and respect for the process. He may need to sell ("positively reinforce") the lessons learned along the way, and the insights yielded through discussion. A related set of issues revolve around Henry's cluelessness. He needs to be much more alert to the dynamics of classroom interaction. Being alert is itself the result of a process of preparation by the instructor: knowing the students and the teaching material very well, anticipating or envisioning the process of each case discussion, clarifying his goals for each class and for the course, and simply preparing his perceptual abilities with a little quiet time before each class. This process of preparation is non-trivial and is easily sacrificed by instructors who have other priorities in their lives. Finally, Henry should remember that how he ends the course can help create the sustainable reputation that can make his job a little easier the next time he opens the course—here, too, he needs to sell the students on how the value proposition has come true, learning has taken place, goals have been met.

- **Longer term.** First, Henry should reflect on whether his heart is in this teaching assignment. Certainly, there is some objective evidence of a mismatch between his research interests or strengths, and the focus of the course. Of course, Henry may have no choice in the matter. But as I have argued elsewhere, passion for the subject is a fundamental driver of good teaching. Second, Henry should consider opportunities to build credibility for himself and the course in advance of the next offering. He might look for opportunities to describe the value proposition of the course more clearly in the syllabus. And he should consider ways to elevate the value proposition that raise credibility: the use of expert outside speakers, the selection of readings and assignments with a strong application orientation, the inclusion of team project assignments that emulate the challenges of actual work life and whose products might become trophies that students could discuss in job interviews.

Conclusion

Professor James Gentry described to me seven attributes displayed by excellent teachers that surfaced in his research on the subject:

1. creates intellectual excitement.
2. establishes great interpersonal rapport.
3. spontaneity, takes the teaching moment and develops it.
4. exudes confidence.
5. takes charge.
6. takes risks in expressing ideas.
7. shows intuitive empathy, is sensitive to what is going on in the classroom.

Henry Domhoff violated every attribute on this list. Fortunately, he can turn the situation around. At the moment where the case ends, he should take action to do so immediately.

Chapter 35
Reprise of Chapter 3: Elizabeth Kent

Elizabeth faces a nasty cluster of problems. First, she admits she is getting angry, an emotion that comes naturally to professionals under stress but that is poison to the relations between professor and student. She has interrupted the discussion twice, each of which sends a strong signal about the appropriateness of the discussion; it won't take much longer for the students to get the message and shut down. In one of these instances, she took one side of the debate, a useful tactic to promote learning but a risky tactic to change direction of the discussion. Nothing she does is working; no wonder she is angry.

Second, she seems to have planned rather ambitiously. The course is on a tight time-schedule, probably with a great deal to cover in a short period of time. In addition, her planning for today's class entailed using 20 minutes of class time for a wrap-up lecture which means that students would have 70, not 90, minutes to discuss the case. These flags suggest that Elizabeth has a problem setting realistic goals for a given class.

Third, she seems to be a captive of her own expertise. She has eight, not five, closing slides. And she has "quite a lot to say to the students on the subject." In her present mind-set, she is focusing on teaching, not learning. She is frustrated that students are not addressing what *she* wanted to discuss. At the same time, an objective observer would see students debating substantial ideas, drawing in personal experiences, generating energy for the subject, and taking charge of their own learning—isn't this the kind of discussion that many instructors would love to have?

Fourth, the students themselves may not be as rigorous as Elizabeth believes them to be, if she has to challenge them to run the numbers. Is she really as in touch with them as she should be?

The origins of this cluster of problems are several:

- She has overlearned the subject of the day. She is a captive of her expertise. With great clarity about the wide range and depth of learning opportunities, she wants to cover it all, or most of it. The result is a supply-driven teaching plan for the day.

- She is trying to do too much. Elizabeth sounds like a bit of a perfectionist, setting very high standards, making high demands, and getting angry when the world fails to rise to them.

- She may have brought some stress into the classroom with her. See Chapter 12 ("Teaching as Theatre") for a discussion of creating some prep time and space before beginning to teach.

The very first agenda item for Elizabeth in the time that remains is to keep her cool. Second, the students seem to be actively engaged in a learning exercise, so she should follow the energy and help the students come to some closure on the issues they have raised in the class.

After class, Elizabeth should make some notes for the next time she teaches the case about what the students saw in it, the points they raised, and where they got especially energized. If the learning points she had targeted are absolutely vital to the success of the next class sessions, Elizabeth might e-mail the students a short expository note on the points, followed by a 10-minute opening discussion of the next class that points out the economics of debt tax shields and their relevance to other possible cases.

Before the next class, Elizabeth should take a hard look at the learning objectives in each of her forthcoming classes. Can they be accomplished realistically? Perhaps she should scale them back. As a practical matter, students will retain two or at most three major points from any case discussion. Trying to load in more learnings will only frustrate teacher and students.

Trying to do too much is a classic trap for well-trained, highly intelligent, ambitious, and perfectionistic professionals. Elizabeth ought to take a reality check on her aims for the course. To the extent that she is stressed out from other activities, she needs to find a way to remain calm in the classroom.

Chapter 36
Reprise of Chapter 4: Eduardo Mendez

Eduardo seems to have forgotten one of the central truths of education: *students learn best that which they teach themselves.* His course offers several contrary tell-tales:

- **Passivity** rather than activity. The breadth and depth of student participation in class discussions is low. About 15 percent of the students actually speak any given day. Students wait for the answer from him rather than derive it on their own.

- **Dullness** rather than alertness. The students show no sparkle, no sense of humor, no energy for the discussions, and no particular engagement with the process.

- **Rote learning** rather than flexible learning. Students want the "right" answer rather than a way of thinking. They seem unable to recognize and solve simple variations in a standard problem.

- **Plagiarism** rather than originality. Representing someone else's work as your own and without attribution corrodes trust, self-respect, and learning.

- **Focus on getting a grade** rather than getting an education.

Eduardo's course is deteriorating into a *mindless* learning experience.

The central question is, What is Eduardo's role in creating this mess? It might be tempting to shed part of the blame onto the learning environment at World University. World seems not to have much of a learning *community* among students. The acid test for the existence of such a community is the existence of strong norms that guide behavior. One notes the weak honor system, anomie, absence of team-based learning, and generally low rate of discussion participation as symptoms of an *institutional malaise.* But blaming World University is too easy. Each year, around the world, instructors at institutions just like World University create vibrant learning communities *within their classrooms.* What has Eduardo done to enable this possibility?

Each of the bullet points that Eduardo cites as evidence of a problem in his course suggest instructor behaviors inconsistent with a student-centered mindful-learning point of view.

- He seems to accept World University's anomie as a ground-rule in his course. He does nothing to organize the course in a way to create its own learning community. The syllabus is silent on the need for participation. He does nothing to organize study teams. Worst of all, he does not know his own students very well.

- It is not clear that he offers a very compelling value proposition to students. Evidently, neither he nor his syllabus sell the course with any enthusiasm, or makes the case for strong learning through discussion. Sure, he allocates 50 percent of the course grade to participation. But plainly students need more of an incentive to participate than the risk of a bad grade—most people feel a need to be a part of something larger and more important. It does not seem that Eduardo has tried to help students *make meaning* out of their work in the course.

- He gives very direct answers to questions. Consider the irony here: in case method courses, the role of the discussion leader is to ask questions calibrated to guide student learning. Instead, Eduardo has allowed the roles to be reversed: students ask, and he answers. No wonder he feels exhausted; he *is* doing all the work.

- He distributes case solutions. This has a number of adverse effects. First it destroys any incentive for students to "learn best that which they teach themselves." Second, it reinforces the notion that there *is* one "right" answer to a case problem. No wonder students pester him for clarity about the right answer. In truth, there is no single "right" answer to a case study (in the sense of a solution that dominates all others), but there may be many wrong answers. Third, it robs students of wrestling with ambiguity, the reality that much in professional life is unknowable and uncertain. It is only through dealing with ambiguity that one can hope to develop mature judgment. Thus Eduardo's practice sacrifices a major opportunity to take students beyond mere technical mastery and into wisdom.

- He has entered negotiation mode on grading. Word is out among students that Eduardo will lift grades on the recent quiz out of sympathy for confusion students might have experienced. This undercuts credibility students may have had in Eduardo's grading: the grade you get is not based on what you know, but on how hard you complain.

- He has neglected personal maintenance. He is tired, which is an undesirable foundation for making wise judgments about teaching and course design. A single person at a large impersonal school, he has no apparent personal support system: no mentor, no circle of peers, no friends with whom he might speak intelligently about the situation.

One could extend the list, but these points are sufficient to suggest that Eduardo has been his own worst enemy. In the very near term, he should consider doing the following:

1. **Take charge.** This entails expressing a sense of command over the daily class discussions, specifically framing questions, rather than statements, as the mode of his leadership. This may require more daily preparation than he has been giving. And he should redirect his overconfidence in his mastery of the cases toward how well the students show *their* mastery of the cases.

2. **Rewrite the rules.** Anomie is a choice, not a given. Eduardo can *choose* whether to buy into the culture of World University or shape his own. But by now, we know what the World University culture offers; the question practically is, What new classroom culture will Eduardo choose to shape? He should require the formation of student study groups. He should work hard to get to know the students (through questionnaires and meetings, either one-on-one or study teams), and then tailor the course in real time in response to what he has learned about them.

3. **Stop handing out solutions.** He needs to explain why solutions degrade student learning. He might possibly go a step further, and ask individuals or teams to hand in written analyses in advance of class discussion.

4. **Stand firm on changes in quiz grades.** Unless faced with an objective error on his part (as in computing point totals), he needs to stop negotiating. He should announce his policy to the class and explain it. On the other hand, he should not close the door to student questions about the quiz—indeed, to deal with the line of students outside his door, he might offer to hold a brown-bag lunchtime quiz review for them. Assuming he wrote a fair quiz, reasonable students will accept his judgment, once they understand it.

5. **Speak with the students, in class, about the low rate and quality of discussion contribution.** The tone of his conversation should not be defensive or scolding: he needs to listen carefully. This may summon up a range of excuses, but most students will respect the effort to find out what is going on. It is vital for this conversation to get positive closure: (1) Eduardo needs to state clearly his expectations about good preparation and active participation; (2) Eduardo may need to cheerlead a little such as, "If we all pull together, we can accomplish great things in this course. Will you join me?" To the extent that Eduardo can identify any opinion leaders in class, he should talk with them individually to sell the value proposition of the course and enlist their support.

6. **Fight *de facto* plagiarism.** Eduardo should speak out against using downloaded solutions as the basis for class participation. He needs to explain that this is equivalent to plagiarism. Students should stop the practice. In addition to the moral argument, he should remind students that "you learn best that which you teach yourself." The opportunity to use these solutions arises in part because of Eduardo's dependence on old, "classic" cases. He should insert a few brand-new cases into the course right now and seriously consider finding much more new material for the next edition of the course.

7. **Talk the talk**: explain repeatedly the need to prepare and participate and the benefits of the discussion method.

8. **Attend to himself.** Eduardo needs to find an alter ego and get some rest. The turnaround of his course will require inner resources and a basis for reflection that he seems not to have at this time. He needs someone with whom he could brainstorm an action plan, check appropriateness of wording, and think two or three steps ahead.

Chapter 37
Ten Ideas for Long Term Development

"Eighty percent of the art of life is showing up."
-- Woody Allen

Someone asked Henry Fonda to offer a sound bite for the most important thing that a young actor should know. Fonda replied, "How to become an old actor." In the highly competitive world of the theatre, becoming an old actor involves more than just showing up for work. There is no guarantee of getting a booking. The critics have a short memory about successes, and a long memory for failures. To approach each new role afresh takes energy and inspiration. In this light, Woody Allen's famous quip is awful advice for the development of professionals. Markets for professional talent do not give much weight simply to showing up. Consider the experience of baseball player, Cal Ripken, who played 2,632 consecutive games over a 20-year career, setting a new record. What the fans celebrate about him is not simply that he "showed up" but that he played *consistently well* enough for the coaches to put him in the game time after time. The relevant question for teachers is how to achieve a similar kind of consistency. Renewal involves more than getting a good night's sleep or mastering basic classroom techniques. If it were easy, we would all be Cal Ripkens in our respective subjects. The challenge must be in what to renew, and how. Crafting a *process* of self-renewal and growth is at the heart of becoming an old actor, an old baseball player, and an old teacher. Previous chapters have emphasized that great professionals carry a learning attitude into their work, and fasten onto interesting variations as exercises in maintaining a keen edge. This chapter offers a "top ten" list of experiences a teacher can use to renew and grow over time.

1. **Team-teach.** Control and consistency of message are relatively easy to achieve when you are the only star in the classroom. But admitting a second star creates a special opportunity to strengthen your capacity to listen, plan, and explain. I'm not talking about one-off special speakers or visitors, people who won't have to clean up after the problems they make. Real team teaching is co-ownership of an entire course, including the determination of grades and the receipt of teaching evaluations. Excellent delivery by a team is very hard to achieve. Students may notice interruptions, disagreements, and differences in intellectual stances, chalkboard styles, idioms, language, and values. The differences will feel uncomfortable, if not threatening to the instructors. Coordination costs will seem

high. But in my experience, students relish this kind of teaching. More importantly, team-teaching is an excellent means for learning new techniques, perceiving your own bad habits, and generally for broadening your repertoire. Everything starts with finding a willing accomplice: pick carefully. Choose a co-teacher on the basis of what you want to learn, rather than what is safe. Also select a colleague whose teaching capabilities you respect and who seems to be a reasonable team player. Next, prepare to deal with bureaucratic resistance. Most schools are not set up for team-teaching; compensation levels assume just one instructor in the room at any time. But a few areas are more receptive to team-teaching designs—executive education, multidisciplinary electives, and special "program events" such as simulations, competitions, and exercises. Third, agree with your colleague on the overarching objectives for the course and on teaching materials. Here's where the differences in disciplines and past experiences will have a big influence on your own learning. Finally, it helps to have some agreement on classroom process: which instructors will stand at the front of the room (one, two, all?) Who is assigned to which topics? And how will the class session achieve closure? It is possible that a team of instructors who are really familiar with each other will leave things vague, but, for novices, it helps to have some dance-steps mapped out. In the case of solo teaching, all of this planning and coordination takes place in the teacher's head. Some people may be able to replicate for themselves the rich dialogue between two colleagues planning a course. But most of us benefit from having a live alter ego who can challenge, prod, help, and celebrate. The coordination of team-teaching is an end in itself.[130]

2. **Write some of your own teaching material.** With so many textbooks and so little time, it may seem that one's value-added is in the classroom rather than composing cases, exercises, problems, technical notes, or other handouts. But the fact is that each teacher conveys a highly personalized view: an emphasis on concepts and how they might be applied to real life. Written materials help crystallize your own view of the subject matter. What makes the preparation of teaching materials a challenge is that you must confront the varieties of ways in which students engage materials. Your initial efforts will show gaps, inconsistencies, and the occasional howling error. Discover these and use them to produce versions 2.0 and beyond. Grow as a teacher as you write.

3. **Teach outside your specialty.** The famous socialist slogan was, "Man is what he eats." Academicians certainly are defined by their intellectual diet. But over the

---

[130] For an illuminating discussion of the issues in team-teaching, see the essay, "Anatomy of a Colleagueship," by Marcy Crary and Duncan Spelman in *Researchers Hooked on Teaching*, Rae Andre and Peter J. Frost eds., Thousand Oaks, CA: Sage Publications 1997.

course of years, a specialty can get confining. Real intellectual or practical life is not bound by academia's definitions. For instance, finance overlaps with accounting and economics. To the sophisticate, the sub-specialties within these fields seem far apart. Nevertheless, neighboring fields often have a lot to contribute to one's understanding of a core area of interest.

4. **Teach outside your country.** This is a big leap. One's Dean, family, and friends may resist at first. One needs an invitation from a foreign school. And the financial outcomes need to meet basic expectations[131], though in the U.S., grants from agencies such as the Fulbright Program[132] can improve the financial attractiveness of teaching abroad. The prime reason for doing this is to engage the challenge of *cultural difference* between you and your students. If you are thoughtful about it, foreign teaching will sharpen your ability to listen to students, structure assignments, evaluate performance, and lead discussions. In short, it will make you better at everything you do in the classroom.

5. **Mentor a colleague.** Academia has been described as the "lonely crowd." Teachers do a miserable job of giving or asking for help. But as several of these chapters attest, *conversation about the task* helps immensely in achieving competence and excellence. Many needy colleagues know they have a thing or two to learn. Most knowledgeable colleagues hold back unnecessarily until they are asked or, worse, until a crisis looms. Be proactive. Set an example and approach other effective teachers to join you in creating a supportive mentoring culture at your school. It may well be that the mentor learns more about teaching skills than does the mentee.

6. **Help a really lost student get back on track.** The emphasis here is on *really.* The lostness may be due in part to the subject matter of your course. But it probably extends to other courses, the desire to be in school at all, or even more ultimate questions. You may feel inadequate to the task. Like it or not, a teacher is *given* these opportunities; one cannot seek them. The best advice is to listen very hard. It is often a defining moment that the student will remember for the rest of his or her life, and that can provide the fulcrum for a personal transformation. What starts as an expression of confusion about the course blossoms into the discovery of a learning disability, an emotional problem, or a genuine threat in the student's life. Often, the best a teacher can do is to help the student find professional assistance focused on the problem—often this requires initiative on

---

[131] Don't get greedy. Pay scales outside of the U.S. are typically lower. Settle for financial break-even, and expect to get large benefits in other ways. Sometimes a successful first experience will translate to economically attractive follow-on work.

[132] For information on the Fulbright Program, visit http://www.iie.org/fulbright/.

the part of the teacher and some wholehearted follow-up to nudge the student along. You will know very quickly how effective you were; but the learning continues for quite a while afterward. Episodes such as these will stimulate over time serious reflection about listening.

7. **Help to turn around a disastrous core course.** Required degree courses are often called "flagships" because they lead the way for students entering the field for the first time. Flagships occasionally sink. Because they are owned by everybody, often they are managed by nobody. When these courses turn sour they reverberate throughout the rest of the program. Sinking flagships are hard to hide. Schools need leaders to return them to smooth sailing. Begin by shedding opportunities to lay blame. The community needs repair, and you may be given the chance to build the community by rebuilding the course. The big hurdles are denial and defensiveness. Often, there isn't complete ownership of the problem. And even when there is, the relevant parties are quite touchy. The key step is to help the faculty get past the failure. Often this amounts to helping them see the long perspective and to recognize that the recent disaster is simply a step in the process of experimentation and improvement. Sometimes one must gain the endorsement of a Dean or other official who will support the turnaround and emphasize that experimenters are not to be shot but, rather, celebrated. Of course, happy talk never suffices: one must confront candidly what went wrong and why. Then one must begin a process to change what must be changed and to hold on to what is good. This is necessarily a consultative effort and gives lessons about advocacy and community building.

8. **Serve your school in an administrative capacity.** Most people enter an academic career because they want to write and teach. Administrative work seems retrograde: scheduling, hiring, planning, cajoling, and rejecting. But administration deepens one's understanding about important drivers of classroom success, such as infrastructure, incentives, loads, professional development, evaluation, promotion, training, and listening. Of special value to your development as a teacher would be assignments to coordinate degree programs and executive programs. If you are creative about the terms of such an assignment, you can maintain some forward momentum in other aspects of your professional life. Good administrative work is an opportunity to teach by different means—structure these assignments to be teaching experiences. Seek administrative service when it is right for you (usually after gaining tenure) and right for the school. Agree with the Dean on a targeted length of service and get it in writing. Set reasonable goals and expectations. Move along when the administrative assignment assumes a routine feeling.

9. **Teach through serving the profession.** This is another exercise in teaching by alternative means. Through professional organizations, you can help to elevate consciousness about teaching and classroom issues. It is gratifying to find professionals at other schools who share similar interests and are willing to reflect with you and others on the state of the art. The two classic avenues of service include conference planning and editorial work for education-oriented journals. Take the initiative to volunteer. What you will gain is greater clarity about teaching issues and practices and a personal network among those interested in teaching.

10. **Stand up for quality of student learning.** Sooner or later in one's professional life, the environment serves up inflection points by which institutions evolve: hiring and promotion decisions, curriculum reforms, school expansions, and so on. Usually, these are defining moments in the life of the school, and surface deeper issues. Frequently, the still small voice in such discussions concerns the learning experience of the students. Speak up on its behalf. You may be alone. The message may be unpopular. You may not be overly confident in your own teaching abilities. The issue at hand may be weighted with political baggage. The stance may be doomed from the outset. But the passage of time often proves such pleadings to be immensely important. The message is an end in itself. However unpopular it may be in the crisis, it proves to be a lasting satisfaction. What one learns from this experience is greater clarity about *why* one seeks to teach well.

One could extend the list further. But these suggestions suffice to make the point that professional renewal and growth reside not in steadily cutting a deeper rut but in periodically stepping off the beaten path. This lends fresh perspective, new feasible solutions to regular problems, and insights that can prepare one for unseen new problems. The "aha" in these suggestions is that one may find renewal where one least expects it. Such experiences, however, are hardly the formula for the easy life. Indeed, they tell us that renewal to become "an old teacher" is risky and is a matter of managing a process of personal challenge and growth. It is not simply "showing up" that counts, but rather it is showing up with consistently good performance. Experiences such as these can help refresh the teacher's skills so that, over a lifetime, consistently good performance is achieved.

Chapter 38
In Closing

In the preface, I asserted that this book was a mosaic of ideas from which if you step back, you see the outlines of a philosophy of student centered discussion leadership. Here are an assortment of "tiles" from which the mosaic is formed:

1. Ask often, tell seldom. All knowledge begins with a question.

2. Hang on to your humility. It is a strong tactic for engaging the student. And besides, you don't know everything.

3. Think like a learner. Focus on learning, not teaching.

4. Aim to build technical mastery *and* wisdom in your students.

5. Emphasize action-taking. Encourage students to take a stand on their ideas.

6. Ideas have consequences. Critically appraise the ideas you teach, and form views about your field based on personal research in it.

7. Your views are vitally important, but let them whisper through discussion leadership and course design.

8. Know the students.

9. Envision discussion processes. Use your imagination as one guide to identify learning opportunities in discussions.

10. Insist on mindfulness.

11. Get dramatic.

12. Display warmth and humor.

13. Watch other good teachers.

14. Learn from criticism of your work and from your mistakes.

15. Use new technology to the extent it can help. But continue to focus on teacher-student engagement.

16. Help a colleague learn about discussion leadership.

17. Tell a story in your course and in each class.

18. Repeat ideas.

19. Invoke student teamwork but set it up carefully.

20. To open a course, focus on forging a classroom "contract."

21. Build active discussions through a good classroom environment, "sticky" ideas, and thoughtful stimulation of thought-leaders.

22. Be tough. But adjust toughness to the students and your learning objectives.

23. Offer closure that promotes ongoing reflection and learning.

24. Set reasonable expectations for work.

25. Keep careful participation records and grade with integrity.

26. Teaching is fundamentally a process of helping students make meaning. Many of the challenges in teaching spring from doubts about meaning.

27. Take on new challenges to continue learning.

Can you see the outlines of what it means to lead discussions in a way that is centered on the student? You may find that certain items in the list are irrelevant or impractical to your situation as a discussion leader. And the list may exclude other issues of vital importance to your situation. I leave it for a later edition or other writers to improve and extend the mosaic. But why wait to flesh out this philosophy? Your next steps should be to *make your own meaning about student centered discussion leadership.*

Some next steps

How can one create some lasting personal momentum around student centered teaching? What to do next will depend on your circumstances. Let me assume that you have the luxury of a little time to reflect, as if during a summer or winter break.

- **Take stock.** A process of change always begins with *you.* Many of the chapters in this book emphasize the importance of self-assessment and reflection. Review the notes you may have made to yourself about your past teaching experiences. Talk with people who may have observed your teaching. Re-read teaching evaluations for the past 2-3 years—perhaps even discuss them with a mentor or sympathetic but honest friend. Privately or in a workshop setting, sketch out what your teaching portfolio statement would look like. At the end of all this, you should ideally emerge with two lists—things you are doing well and things you would like to improve—and a sense of renewed commitment and purpose.

- **Redesign.** Some of the teaching crises of the moment have seeds in course design or materials selection decisions made months earlier. There is no better time than the lull between teaching assignments to tinker with all elements of a course. Look for new teaching materials—students always welcome fresh case studies, and current events will dictate a shifting focus over time. Check out the syllabi of instructors at other schools; many of these are on websites available to the public. Contact one or two of these instructors to discuss their course designs—if they are nearby, meet with them in person. Drill down into the ideas to form your own opinion. This may entail comparing the messages in different textbooks, reading the primary articles, or even doing your own original research. As Chapter 4 emphasized, the sense of discovery associated with this can summon extra enthusiasm and possibly new insights about how to present the material. At the end of all this, you should have a syllabus that outlines the objectives of the course, design, and daily assignments.

- **Read.** In parallel with the first two steps, one could dip into the literature on discussion leadership and learning. A number of recommended readings are cited in footnotes and reference lists throughout this book. This kind of reading deepens ones frame of thinking about discussion leadership and sparks new insights about one's own strengths and weaknesses.

- **Observe.** Find some exemplars in discussion leadership, and watch them teach over four or five class sessions. Use the kinds of disciplined techniques outlined in Chapter 14 or any other framework you find useful. Just remember that one wants to see, and not merely look. This will be time-consuming. If you consider your own preparation for each class, the actual class time, and post-class discussion, you are committing 15 to 20 hours of discretionary time. But done well, this can yield a wealth of insights about teaching materials, discussion leadership techniques, classroom culture, etc.

- **Talk with friends, coach, mentor.** You need one or more people with whom you can talk regularly, casually, sympathetically, and honestly, about discussion leadership. Look for those who love to teach, to discuss, to explore. Avoid cynics, diehard lecturers, and know-it-alls. Take the risky first step: offer to buy them lunch or coffee, and see where the conversation heads. Like a good discussion leader, carry a couple of objectives in mind for each conversation but don't be directive. Let yourself be surprised by serendipity. The mini-cases in this book, and other short resource materials could be used to spark discussion. Take the opportunity to encourage others in skills of discussion leadership. You will learn as you teach others.

- **Teach.** Effective questioning, listening, and responding are learned through practice. Enter class each day with a clear focus on the students and what you are trying to accomplish with them. Make notes after each class about what went well, and what didn't. To the extent possible record the layout of the chalkboard—this can yield valuable tips to help you prepare for class the next time you teach the material. Invite a colleague or mentor to observe your teaching, and give comments. Have your teaching videotaped and watch the tape.

- **Repeat the cycle.** This kind of investment really works. The second time around will seem easier since the infrastructure you built, and momentum you gained, will serve to boost your mastery and self-confidence as a discussion leader.

Through these "next steps" you become your own teaching muse: creative, critical, reflective, and inspiring to others. Such an outcome is surely one of the highest aims of education.